THE HISTORY OF
Browning Firearms

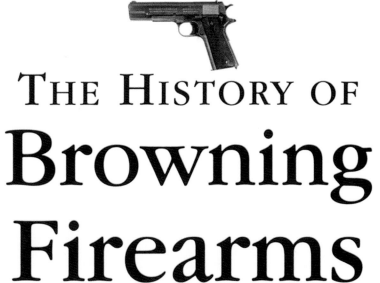

THE HISTORY OF
Browning
Firearms

**A Complete Chronicle of
the Greatest Gunsmith of All Time**

David Miller

Skyhorse Publishing

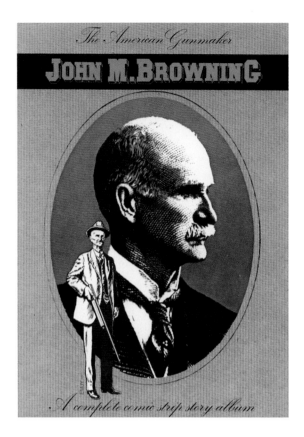

The American Gunmaker

JOHN M. BROWNING

A complete comic strip story album

Skyhorse Publishing books may be purchased in bulk at special discounts for sales promotion, corporate gifts, fund-raising, or educational purposes. Special editions can also be created to specifications. For details, contact the Special Sales Department, Skyhorse Publishing, 307 West 36th Street, 11th Floor, New York, NY 10018 or info@skyhorsepublishing.com.

Skyhorse® and Skyhorse Publishing® are registered trademarks of Skyhorse Publishing, Inc.®, a Delaware corporation.

Visit our website at www.skyhorsepublishing.com.

10 9 8 7 6 5 4 3 2 1

Library of Congress Cataloging-in-Publication Data is available on file.

Above: The album that was published in 1978 by Fabrique Nationale Herstal (FN) in commemoration of the one hundredth anniversary of the Browning company.

Page 1: The Browning facility at Morgan, Utah.

Print ISBN: 978-1-5107-5653-3
Ebook ISBN: 978-1-5107-5680-9

Printed in China

CONTENTS

Introduction

Above: The famous 'Four B's' – G. L. Becker, John M. Browning, A. P. Bigelow and Matthew S. Browning. During the 1890's these four Ogdenites were Utah's premier live-bird team. Later they made national history at the traps as a squad of four.

Above: Browning's Gun Store in Ogden, Utah.

JOHN MOSES BROWNING (1855–1926) is widely acknowledged to be one of the greatest firearms designers of all time; indeed, many would describe him as the greatest. His father, Jonathan Browning (1805–1879) was a gunsmith and designed several unusual rifles, but was simply not in the same league as his son, whose output included 128 patents and at least 80 separate designs.

John and his brothers lived in the tiny frontier town of Ogden, Utah which was "Old West" country and linked to the Eastern states by long and tenuous roads and trails, and from 1869 by the railroad. Despite such relative isolation and leaving school at fifteen after a typical rural education, John became a very respected businessman, first on a national scale, dealing with such well-established companies as Colt, Remington, Stevens and Winchester, and later on the international stage, regularly traveling to Europe to visit his closest business partner, Fabrique Nationale of Liége, Belgium. He also became closely involved with the United States government and with the army and navy, whose officers treated him with the greatest respect.

Browning's designs covered the whole range of small arms, from semi-automatic pistols, through single-shot rifles and many different types of repeater rifles to machine guns. His brain was constantly active and he conducted a never-ending search for perfection. One of his greatest assets was that he was a highly enthusiastic shot and practiced his skills not only on ranges and in competitions, but also in the hills, fields and forests around Ogden, where he was able to loose off thousands of rounds from each weapon, detecting and analysing shortcomings and devising remedies which could then be implemented immediately in the workshop.

In writing about the Browning story, it is important to stress that the workshop in Ogden was not a firearms production facility. The shop sold and repaired hardware, such as farming implements and tools, and the firearms business was confined to making and refining John's prototypes, and to selling and repairing firearms which had been produced elsewhere. Apart from weapons designed by the father, Jonathan Browning, and, as will be explained, the first 600 of John's Single-Shot Rifles, only prototypes of Browning weapons were made there. When John sold his designs to other companies, he also gave up the right to manufacture them.

John Browning's designs were made under license by both U.S. and foreign firearms companies, but there have also been many "clones" which are exact copies of Browning weapons, although all too often made to far less rigorous engineering standards.

John Moses Browning collapsed and died in his office at the Fabrique Nationale factory in Liége, Belgium, in 1926. He was surrounded by many of his family and by workers whom he respected, in a factory whose fortunes he had done so much to secure. It was a fitting end to the life of a truly great man.

Salt Lake City, Utah in the 1850s was still the "Old West" when John M. Browning was growing up.

CHAPTER ONE

John Moses Browning – An American Hero

THE BROWNING FAMILY arrived in Virginia in the 1620s and remained there for well over one hundred years. John Moses Browning's grandfather, Edmund Browning, was born there in 1761, but in his twenties he married and he and his bride then joined the trek westwards, settling in Brushy Fork, Tennessee, where his wife gave birth to seven children. One of those children, Jonathan, was born in October 1805, but unlike his father, his interest was in blacksmithing and tanning rather than farming. Jonathan found his first work in a local smithy and then, at age 19, he went to Nashville, Tennessee, to work for a gunsmith in order to learn the highly specialized art of making and truing barrels, a vital skill in a society where virtually every family had at least one gun and used them to shoot for the pot or for self-defense.

Jonathan Browning returned to Brushy Fork, where he established his own business and married, but the work fell away as their neighbors answered the siren call of the West. In 1833 Jonathan and his family joined them, heading westwards and eventually finding a new home in Quincy, Illinois on the banks of the Mississippi.

In 1842 Jonathan made a fundamental change to his and his family's way of life, by converting to the Mormon religion, whereupon they moved to Nauvoo, Illinois where he once again set up a new gunmaking business. Jonathan repeatedly volunteered to join his co-religionists in their march to the West but his church authorities told him that he was needed in Nauvoo and to continue to make arms. His persistence finally triumphed, however, and in 1852 he moved with his family to Ogden in Utah, some 30 miles from Salt Lake City. There he took a second wife and then a third, having an eventual total of 22 children, the last of whom was born when he was 71 years old. Jonathan was a respected member of the community, becoming a local councilor and judge, but always retaining his gunsmithing business, although he never made a new gun after the move to Utah, concentrating instead on repair

Jonathan Browning

work. In his earlier years he designed a repeating rifle using a horizontally sliding, four-round magazine, which worked well, but it was designed for use with percussion caps and had the ill luck to appear just as metallic cartridges appeared. Jonathan died in 1879 at the age of 74.

John Moses Browning

John Moses Browning was the eldest of two sons of Jonathan Browning's second wife and was born in Ogden, Utah, on January 23, 1855. By the age of six he was regularly helping his father in the workshop and a year later he was also

working in the tannery. He made his first gun at the age of ten, creating a rifle to his own design from components he found among his father's piles of scrap, and which he then used to shoot prairie chicken for the family table. He also repaired farm machinery, and, when driven by necessity, made moccasins and boots. When just past his thirteenth birthday he was given a broken but high-quality shotgun by one of his father's customers and his first action was to disassemble it down to the smallest possible component. He analyzed every part, repaired or replaced those that were damaged and ended up with a thoroughly usable gun, of far higher quality than he would have been able to afford at that stage in his life.

The town of Ogden was an isolated Western outpost – a small Mormon community in outback Utah. The first major change came when the trans-continental railroad was completed in 1869, with the famous "Golden Spike" episode actually taking place only 50 miles away. The second, even more crucial change came in January 1870 when the Utah Central Railroad gave Ogden a direct link to Salt Lake City and thus to the outside world.

John attended the local school which was a typical Western school with one teacher supervising a number of classes in one large room. John certainly learned to read and write and do arithmetic, but he had probably learned little more than that, and when the teacher told him that he had nothing more to pass on to his pupil they both realized that it was time for John to leave.

John's early days in the workshop were, not surprisingly, devoted to perfecting his skills, and he worked hard at repairing guns, although his enquiring mind and detailed examination of the various mechanisms that came his way led him to devise methods of improving them. Nevertheless, he did not move on into the realm of real invention until 1878, when, at 23, he finally got down to designing a totally new gun, which was destined to become the famous Single-Shot. As would happen repeatedly over the coming years, he prepared the whole concept, both in detail and in its totality, in his mind, before preparing drawings and then starting work on the prototype, the whole process taking him about eleven months. This was an incredible achievement, firstly because it was his very first design and secondly because he achieved in just under a year what it takes most people about five to complete.

Despite living in a remote Western town and his limited knowledge of the ways of the world, John knew that he had to protect his work with a patent, but had no idea how to go about it. Undeterred, he turned to a mail-order company in the East whose goods he sold in the shop and they, very courteously, passed his query to a patent attorney. The latter treated the application with the

In 1852 Jonathan Browning and his family moved west along the Mormon trail.

Nauvoo, Illinois

ORIGINALLY NAMED COMMERCE, the Mormons renamed it Nauvoo — meaning a beautiful place of rest in Hebrew. The central building, the Temple, whose cornerstone was laid on April 6, 1841, formed the hub of the community. Within 5 years the town had been established but pressure from the Mormon's neighbors forced them to undertake the vigil West in 1846 to find new freedom from persecution. Jonathan Browning was keen to make the trip West but Mormon leaders recognizing the need for maintaining arms for defense kept him back to repair the community's weapons. Observers who visited the town after it had been deserted reported a place with newly built houses surrounded by well tended gardens.

The town has now been rebuilt and is an historic American Site.

Above: The Browning workshop in reconstructed Nauvoo. Jonathan set up shop here in 1842 after converting to the Mormon religion.

Right: The Browning Homestead adjoins the workshop.

Left: John Moses Browning's parents.

Below : A detail of Jonathan Browning's repeating percussion cap rifle.

Bottom: A revolving rifle made by Jonathan on display in his workshop in Nauvoo.

Above: John Moses Browning aged 18.

Left: Union Pacific locomotive Number 82 and its crew between Echo and Evanston, less than 60 miles from Ogden in 1872, two years after the railroad opened allowing the Brownings direct contact with the Eastern States.

Left Below: A small local school like the one that John attended.

seriousness it deserved, translated the inventor's flowing prose into the correct dry legal terminology and duly obtained U.S. Patent Number 220,271 of 1879, the first of many which would be granted to the Western inventor.

It was during this patent process that Jonathan Browning died, leaving the shop to John, but as he had already been running it for two years the transition was smooth. Indeed, business was booming and John, together with his younger brother and stepbrothers, moved and built new premises. Their first manufactured product was the Browning Single-Shot Rifle and they sold 25 in the first week at $25 each, although they continued with the repair business and also expanded the shop to deal in hunting and sporting goods.

Browning and Winchester

By this stage Ogden, although by no means large, was expanding rapidly, mainly because of its status as a prime junction for the railroad system. The ease of travel and communication was of inestimable value to the Browning brothers' business, which was now in direct railroad contact with the Eastern states. In 1882 John Browning took out two more patents, and by now the

reputation of the Browning Single Shot was spreading, while back in Ogden production proceeded steadily. In 1883, however, came one of those lucky breaks which all inventors need, when one of the Winchester Repeating Arms Company's salesmen chanced on a used Browning Single-Shot Rifle and, immediately recognizing its merits, bought it for $15 and sent it to the Winchester factory. It so happened that Winchester had a serious gap in its product line for such a single-shot rifle and the management board took less than a week to decide to buy the design. Accordingly, they dispatched the general manager, T.G. Bennett, to discover whatever he could about the Browning company, which was totally unknown on the East coast. That the general manager of one of the world's greatest arms companies should personally undertake such a journey is an extraordinary compliment to both John Browning and the quality of his design. Bennett arrived unannounced and found the young brothers busy at their lathes and anvils, but the discussion was short, sharp and to the point, and ended with Bennett writing the letter of understanding on the shop counter.

This first contract between John and the Winchester company granted the latter the sole manufacturing and

The Winchester dynasty: Thomas Gray Bennett, husband of Oliver Winchester's daughter, with his son Winchester Bennett and grandson T.G. Bennett. Thomas was the Vice President of the company responsible for initiating the link with Browning.

sales rights and was for $8,000, making the Brownings fairly rich by the general standard of the times and fantastically rich by local Utah standards. In today's terms the contract would be for between half and one million dollars, depending on the conversion factor used, but by any standard it was a huge amount of money for a tiny company based in remote Ogden.

For Winchester the rifle was a godsend and sales started in 1885. Browning's design was so inherently robust, reliable and adaptable that it was capable of adjustment to take a wide range of cartridges from .50 Winchester Express down to .22 Short. A small problem arose when Bennett discovered that, in all innocence, the brothers were continuing to produce Single-Shots in their own workshop to meet existing orders and he courteously explained that they had transferred all

production rights to him. As with all their contracts with the Brownings, Winchester's policy was to purchase exclusive rights to patents; they never agreed to pay royalties. This may appear one-sided at first glance, but it also had some advantages for John Browning in that on many occasions the company purchased patents which they knew they would not put into production for one reason or another.

With his next design, a lever-action rifle, John Browning decided that this time he would take the prototype rifle to Winchester himself, even though the farthest he and his brother Matt had ever traveled before was 35 miles to Salt Lake City. Now, however, they traveled by trans-continental train to New York City and, after a night seeing the sights, on to New Haven, Connecticut – a journey which in those days took six days. Winchester took one

Above: John M. Browning's workbench at the gunshop in Ogden, Utah.

Left: John M in 1890 when he was beginning his experiments with self-loading firearms.

look at the rifle, realized that it was way ahead of anything anywhere else in the world and bought it immediately, as always with a lump sum rather than royalties, believed in this case to be $50,000.

Having bought the production rights for five guns, now, for the first time, Winchester asked Browning to design a weapon, in this case a lever-action, repeating shotgun. Browning agreed that it was possible but said that he would prefer to produce a slide-action weapon. Browning delivered the prototype in June 1885, Winchester was delighted, tooled-up and entered the weapon in their catalog as the Model 1887. Thus in just three years, John Browning had produced three

Marcellus Hartley, Remington's President, whose death, while Browning was waiting to see him, caused John to offer his automatic shotgun to FN in Belgium.

outstanding designs – the Models 1885, 1886 and 1887 Winchesters.

Set apart

John Browning was a Mormon all his life and when his Church called him in 1887 to undertake two years' missionary work he did not hesitate, despite the fact that he was just starting to make his reputation as a gun designer. In obedience to the call he became a full-time missionary in Georgia, working there from March 1887 to March 1889.

Return to Winchester

John Browning's return to Ogden was followed by a period of exceptional productivity. Sometimes he produced a new design on his own and sometimes he responded to suggestions from Winchester – for example, the Winchester Model 92 was the result of a request from Bennett for an entirely new design built around the .40-40 cartridge, to replace the Model 73. During one of John's visits to New Haven, Bennett offered him $10,000 if a prototype could be ready in three months time, but John delivered it at New Haven within one month, which included both his trip back to Ogden and sending the rifle

to Connecticut, two five-day train journeys. John Browning was paid $20,000 for his efforts, but, even so, that was a tremendous bargain for Winchester who eventually sold over one million copies.

This was a time of accelerating development in the armaments business, and the appearance of smokeless powder in 1894 revolutionized the gunmaking and ammunition fraternities alike. There was some initial resistance but the advantages of the new powder and the rounds it fired were so obvious that weapons were quickly developed to take full advantage of them. Winchester found that all of their production weapons designed by John Browning were easily adapted to accommodate the higher pressures, the first on the scene being the Winchester Model 94 firing the smokeless .30-30 round. Next came the big-game Winchester Model 95, a lever-action box magazine rifle, firing a variety of rounds from .30-02 up to .405. Over the years between 1883 and 1900 Winchester bought 44 rifle and shotgun designs from Browning; not all of them were put into production, but those that were sold phenomenally well. During this period the Winchester patent department dealt with all Browning's patent claims, although he also produced designs which he sold to other companies on a royalty basis.

Meanwhile, Browning's ever-productive mind had been working on automatic weapons and machine guns (see below), but in 1902 he designed the world's first automatic shotgun. Again, the Winchester patent department processed his claim, but Bennett prevaricated for some two years over accepting the design for production. Eventually Browning traveled to New Haven to resolve matters, but, after a short and frigid interview, Browning picked up the prototypes and his relationship with Winchester, which had been so beneficial and profitable for both, was at an end.

A brief encounter with Remington

On leaving the Winchester factory, John Browning immediately made arrangements to meet with Marcellus Hartley, the president of the Remington Arms Company, and at the appointed time presented himself at that company's head office. But, while he was waiting to be called in to Hartley's office, an ashen-faced secretary came to tell him that his chief had just died of a heart attack. Thus, Remington, through ill-fortune rather than ill-management, lost the opportunity to become the sole manufacturer of the Auto-5, although they were to produce it later as the Remington Model 11 for the U.S. market only.

The Belgian arms manufacturer, Fabrique Nationale, had been producing John's automatic pistol for several years and had been trying to persuade him to travel across the Atlantic to Europe. They did not succeed until the

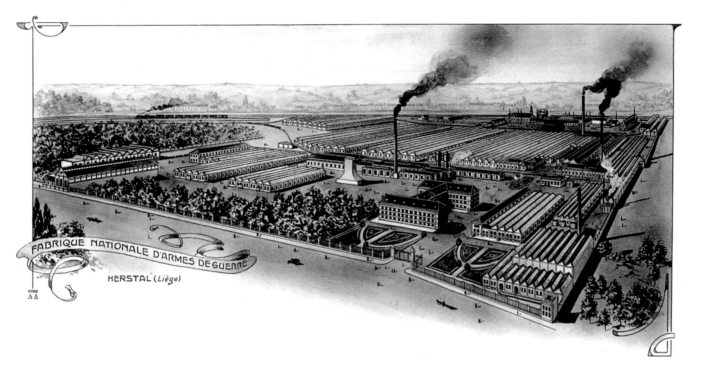

The FN Factory at Herstal in Belgium.

falling-out with Winchester and the death of Remington's president in 1902 persuaded John to offer them his automatic shotgun. He traveled by ocean liner and for the first time found himself outside the company of Americans, especially arms experts, and felt a little isolated as a result. However, he found the time to spend a week in Paris, where he studiously visited all the sights and, as befitted his new status as an international businessman, purchased a number of tailor-made suits.

The visit to Fabrique Nationale was a resounding success. The company was already manufacturing Browning's .32 pistol which was selling well and they were even more delighted with the world's first effective automatic shotgun. A contract was signed on March 24, giving Fabrique Nationale worldwide manufacturing rights in return for royalty payments. Browning stayed for three months to sort out the production details and the workers quickly learned to respect him as a gunsmith and to like him as a man, naming him Le Maître (the master). John Browning showed his own faith in his weapon by placing an order for 10,000 for the U.S. market and every one of them was sold within a year by Schoverling of New York.

Automatic weapons

John Browning first glimpsed the possibilities of a weapon which automatically loaded its next shot in 1889 on a firing range outside Ogden, while watching a rather short man firing a rifle. Browning noticed that when the man fired, a clump of weeds a few feet in front of the muzzle swayed in the blast. His inventor's mind immediately told him that this represented energy which might well be put to productive use and he rushed home to test his theory by securing a rifle to a rest and demonstrating that the muzzle blast caused a wooden board placed near the muzzle to go spinning around the room. That night John designed a rudimentary gas-operated gun in his head and the next day set about building it. This rifle had a "flapper" placed over the muzzle with a hole in it which was marginally greater in diameter than the bore of the barrel. This flapper was pivoted and linked to the mechanism by rods. The prototype was completed by four o'clock that afternoon and proved that the gas could indeed be used to reload the weapon automatically. Its purpose fulfilled, the prototype was discarded, its parts later being used in other experiments, and, sadly, does not survive.

Browning's first patent for an automatic weapon was filed in January 1890 followed by two more in August 1891, a fourth in July 1892 and a fifth in November 1892, all using different mechanisms. John had two problems with his new automatic gun: the first was designing and developing a working prototype; the second was marketing it, since it was clearly only suitable for military use and he had no prior experience of dealing with government arms procurement.

When he judged the first prototype to be ready John

Browning took it to Colt where, to the astonishment of the sophisticated Easterners, he and his brother Matt demonstrated that it could fire four 50-round belts in a minute without a stoppage except to change belts. The demonstration was spectacular and the Colt management spent two days discussing matters with the Brownings, as a result of which some two months later the Brownings demonstrated this new "machine gun" to two officers of the U.S. Navy. These two men then devised an operational requirement for an automatic gun which could fire continuously for three minutes, supposedly simulating an action with two battleships close together and seeking to repel boarding parties.

The requirement was ludicrous in both its tactical setting and in its demand for three minutes' continuous firing, since there was no weapon in the world which could go anywhere near meeting it, but Browning conducted the demonstration in person, with the air-cooled machine gun mounted on a tripod to which he had attached a bicycle seat – a feature which would become standard on virtually every MG throughout the world. By the end the barrel was red hot, but the gun simply kept going and fired 1,800 rounds in three minutes without a single mechanical stoppage, thus fully meeting the requirement. Despite his gun having demonstrated its superiority over the other manually-operated Gatling guns then in service no order was immediately forthcoming, which did at least give Browning the time to convert his gun to take the new smokeless and rimless cartridges with a minimum of fuss and difficulty. After further trials the U.S. Navy classified the weapon as the Colt Model 1895 machine gun, named it the "Peacemaker" and ordered an initial quantity of fifty, which were delivered in 1897. They were in use with the U.S. Marines during the Boxer War in China and in the Spanish–American War, and some were also sold to South American armies.

The Model 1895 was air-cooled, but in 1900 John began work on a water-cooled weapon and in his usual way it took just three months from telling his brothers of the project to a working prototype, which became the father of all subsequent Browning machine gun designs, many of which are still in service over a hundred years later. The weapon is sometimes identified as the Browning Model 1901, but despite numerous successful demonstrations no order or Government type classification was forthcoming. Nevertheless, John kept working on the design, revisiting it at intervals to modify and improve it, although even after the power of tripod-mounted machine guns had been clearly shown in the early years of World War I the U.S. Army Ordnance Department still did not place any orders.

Despite the clear evidence of the importance of large numbers of machine guns in the war, and the ever-growing likelihood of U.S. involvement, the army made no move until February 1917, when the twenty-year old Colt Model 1895 was placed in urgent production. Fortunately, the company had retained the tooling. The delay meant that the U.S. Army went to war with a total machine gun inventory of only some 200 Model 1904 water-cooled Maxims, 670 Benét Mercié air-cooled machine guns, and 185 Colt Model 1895s.

In 1910 Browning had also produced a totally new design of light machine gun, which would become the world-famous Browning Automatic Rifle (BAR), and which, again, impressed the service authorities, but not sufficiently to make them place orders. In April 1917 with an order still in the balance, John Browning fired 20,000 rounds on the official range without any stoppages and then fired a further 20,000. This was such a phenomenal performance that some refused to believe that there had not been some form of trickery (e.g., by switching guns) so Browning repeated the trial with a second gun, but this time under even closer observation, but the same result was achieved. Having determined that it would order Browning's heavy machine gun, automatic rifle and .45 automatic pistol into urgent production, the U.S. Government then sought to negotiate a price with Browning for full manufacturing

The Colt-Browning Model 1895. Its mechanical simplicity made the gun an instant success.

Automatic Pistols

John Browning started work on a semi-automatic pistol in 1894 and his first four attempts were completed in 1895–6 and successfully tested by Colt, who signed a royalty agreement with him in 1896, but for production and marketing in the United States only. Then, in 1897 John was visiting the Colt factory when he chanced to meet Hart O. Berg, an American-born businessman who lived in Belgium where he worked for the Fabrique Nationale d'Armes de Guerre (National Factory of Weapons of War), usually known simply as Fabrique Nationale or FN, and which was located at Liége. The company had been raised by a consortium and the factory built from scratch a few years earlier to manufacture weapons for the Belgian army, but had plenty of spare capacity. When Berg returned to Belgium he took one of Browning's automatic pistols with him and the FN board was so impressed that they quickly negotiated a contract and put it into production as the Browning .32 Model 1900. It was a tremendous success, with half-a-million sold in ten years and in French-speaking countries it became known simply as "le Browning."

One of John Browning's greatest contributions to semi-automatic pistol design was the slide, which covered the barrel and other working parts, as well as supplying the mass necessary to absorb the recoil. In early 1900s he began work on what became the Colt Military Model, with concurrent work on a new .45 round to provide the stopping power needed. The result was submitted to Ordnance tests in 1911 where it was required to: fire a total of 6,000 standard rounds in series of 100 followed by 5 minutes cooling, with cleaning and oiling after 1000 rounds; fire a number of doctored rounds to simulate faulty ammunition which might be met in battle conditions; and pass a "rust-and-dust" test. The

rights for the duration of the war, a deal which would include John's personal supervision of all factories where these weapons were produced. The sum offered was $750,000, a fraction of what he would have been earned under a royalty arrangement, but there were no negotiations, since John knew exactly where his patriotic duty lay and accepted on the spot. He was also offered the rank of colonel, but this he turned down without a second thought.

As soon as U.S. forces were in France they sent back a requirement for a heavy .50 in machine gun. U.S. Army engineers first tried to convert the existing Browning .30 in machine gun to take the heavier French 11 mm round but without success, although the efforts proved to be very time-consuming. So they asked John Browning to design a new heavy automatic gun, which he did with his usual panache and speed, but even he did not have sufficient time and it was already too late to see service in World War I. Known as the Browning .50 it was originally a water-cooled weapon but was later converted by Browning himself to air-cooling, in which form it is still in production in 2006.

Browning pistol passed with flying colors and was, in fact, the first automatic weapon ever to pass government tests with a 100 percent score. The outcome was a production order a pistol which remained in full service with the U.S. military for over 50 years, and which is still in wide-scale use today.

37 mm Cannon

Prior to World War I the U.S. Government tried to develop a 37 mm anti-aircraft cannon, which resulted in two models, both of which failed their tests. After the war, the government asked John Browning to look at the problem; initially he demurred, but eventually agreed. He started work in January 1921 and, in his usual fashion, finished the prototype in just three months; indeed, he was so quick that the government was unable to supply him with any ammunition for the trials. So impatient was Browning for progress that he started his own search and discovered some stock in an army depot only a few miles south of Ogden. The cannon successfully passed stringent Government tests, but Browning was then asked to design a more powerful and higher velocity bullet. So, as always, he persevered and produced, first, a weapon firing a 2,000 ft/sec bullet, and in response to yet further requests another firing a 3,050 ft/sec round. All these weapons passed their tests with flying colors, but the services then found themselves starved of money and with little interest in Congress, so the project was put on hold, with no further progress until well after John's death.

Death

In 1926 John Browning made his sixty-first Atlantic crossing, accompanied by his wife, with the aim of visiting FN and also meeting up with their son, Val, who was resident in Liége. One morning they went into the factory to look at development of a new shotgun, but on arrival John complained of chest pains and was forced to lie down. After only a short period he died – he suffered little, was in a gun factory, at work on one of his designs, and with his wife and son. It was a sad but fitting end to a very great man.

Following John's death production of his various designs continued, with all the family interests controlled, as in his day, from Ogden, but in 1964 the Browning Arms Company moved from Morgan, just a few miles away and still in the state of Utah, where it remains today, located in Cottonwood Canyon, just outside the village of Mountain Green. As it has done since 1885, it continues to buy-in and market firearms, but not to manufacture them, and has also branched out into bows, knives and other sporting goods, together with running a profitable commercial mink ranch.

Fabrique Nationale

FN was badly affected by World War II. The factory had been taken over by the German weapons procurement organization in 1940 and new management was installed so that selected weapons, such as the Model 35 Hi-Power pistol, could be produced for the German armed forces. In 1944, during the final weeks of occupation, the Germans shipped out as much of the production machinery as possible and after they had left attacked the factory with V-1 and V-2 missiles. Even so, production quickly restarted and FN-made Hi-Power pistols were soon being exported to the United States where they were sold under the Browning label.

This relationship between the U.S.-based Browning Arms Company and FN remained unchanged until 1976 when FN, in partnership with Japanese company, B.C. Miroku (see below), purchased 90 percent of the Browning company's shares. The main shareholder in the FN group at this time was a Belgian bank, *la Société Générale de Belgique*, but in 1991 both FN and its U.S. subsidiaries were bought by French state-owned defense giant, GIAT Industries. This arrangement did not last very long and in 1997 the State Government of Wallonia, in which the factory is situated, purchased the Herstal Group for $303 million, bringing ownership back into Belgian hands.

B.C. Miroku

B.C. Miroku, based in Kochi, Japan, started making hunting guns in 1893 and concentrated on the domestic market until undertaking production of military weapons in 1940–45. When it restarted operations in the post-war period, Miroku's products were initially intended, as before, for the Japanese market, but in the early 1960s they began to make weapons to sell on the U.S. market, their first known customer being the Charles Daly company, which had been importing German and Italian weapons for many years. But, in 1976 Miroku combined with FN to buy the Browning Arms Company, whereupon Miroku ceased making guns for Charles Daly and switched to Browning models, with production of various weapons, including the Auto-5 shotgun and the .22 caliber Self-Loading Rifle being transferred from FN to their Japanese partner. Today Miroku has a workforce of some 1,000 people and continues to produce weapons for Browning although it also exports a small, but increasing, number of weapons under its own name. Curiously, although expert opinion is virtually unanimous that the quality of the Miroku-made Brownings is, at the very least, as good as any made by any other manufacturer, U.S.-based firearms collectors tend to rate Miroku guns below U.S.- or Belgian-made guns for collectability, a view which is reflected in their sales prices.

Other makers

Most of the semi-automatic pistols sold in the United States under the Browning label have been (and continue to be) made by FN, but some other models have been sourced elsewhere. The Model BDA-380 (Browning Double Action .38 Caliber), for example, was made for FN by Beretta, Italy from 1977 to 1997, and then marketed in the U.S. by Browning. The similarly named Model BDA, manufactured between 1977 and 1980 for Browning by German/Swiss company, SIG-Sauer, was a totally different design and virtually identical to the SIG-Sauer P-220. It has since been restored to production for the U.S. market, but in .45 caliber only and under the SIG-Sauer (and not the Browning) label. Another company which manufactured weapons for the Browning company in the post-war period is Sako of Rihimaki, Finland, which produced the High-Power Bolt-Action Rifle between 1961 and 1975.

John Browning's life

John Moses Browning was, by any standard, a most remarkable man. Brought up in a remote town in the Old West, his intellect, drive and inventive genius turned him into a world-renowned engineer who earned universal respect and admiration. Those who have had the privilege of working with inventors know that they look at things in a totally different way from the mass of humanity. Most people, on encountering a problem or on seeing a need, either back off or painfully and slowly find a way around. Inventors, on the other hand, are blessed with a mental process which enables them to see their way straight to a solution. Thus, John Browning was able to observe a phenomenon such as the shock wave from a bullet swaying the grass and go straight to its application in an automatic system. Not only that, but he was always able to see solutions in both totality and in detail, right down to the smallest component.

Of course, he was not always right the first time. For example, his "flapper" demonstrated how gas could be used in recocking and reloading a weapon, but it was not a practical solution and turned out to be just one step in the right direction rather than the complete answer. Also, a few of his ideas turned out to be impracticable. In one example, he spent some time in the 1890s on a "pull-apart" mechanism for repeating rifles and although he produced working prototypes, the idea was never accepted. In addition, much additional work was often needed to turn his concepts into weapons which could be mass-produced and sold at a reasonable price and the engineers at Colt, Winchester and Fabrique Nationale worked hard and successfully to achieve this.

One of the keys to his phenomenal success was that he was what would today be called a "hands-on" man,

John M.Browning shortly before his death in 1926.

because he not only designed the weapons but he also built (or helped to build) the prototypes, and then tested them by firing them himself on the ranges and hills outside Ogden. Also, as a regular hunter and participant in shooting competitions he understood guns and the men who fired them. On top of all that he also conducted the business negotiations with prospective manufacturers, even when they were as far away as Belgium. There have been many men who have made significant contributions to the design of weapons and the advance of firearms technology, but none to equal John Moses Browning.

CHAPTER TWO

Self-Loading Pistols

BY THE 1870s THE REVOLVER, with its ammunition held in a rotating cylinder, was well-established and proving itself to be a solid and effective weapon, with a simple mechanical action that was usually reliable in all but the most extreme circumstances. Revolvers made by Colt and by Smith & Wesson in the United States and by Webley and others in the United Kingdom were excellent, and proved their worth in many a shoot-out and campaign. One of the revolver's major limitations, however, was its ammunition capacity, with the great majority of designers settling for six rounds. Some did opt for more – the French Le Mat of 1868, for example, held nine .44 rounds – but anything over six rounds usually resulted in a bulky and increasingly unmanageable weapon.

Shooters wanted more ammunitionion the gun, however, and the answer came in the 1880s with the self-loading or semi-automatic pistol in which the rounds were stored in a magazine fitted into the underside or the butt. Initially, these designers faced some major obstacles, the most intransigent of which was the use of the traditional black powder, which left a large amount of residue to foul the working parts, leading very rapidly to jamming of the automatic mechanism. The second problem was that cartridge cases were rimmed, which not only made for curved magazines, but which also complicated both loading and ejection. Thirdly, the soft lead bullet was often deformed during the chambering process, again causing stoppages.

Fortunately, solutions to all these problems were at hand. First, the invention of smokeless powder solved the fouling problem. Secondly, the removal of the cartridge rim meant that magazines could be straight, although a groove in the case (technically known as a cannelure) then became necessary for the extraction process. Finally, more robust jacketed bullets were designed which withstood the deflections which took place during chambering.

John Moses Browning was fully aware of these

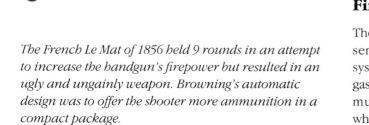

developments and, having gained considerable expertise in the design and construction of gas-operated machine guns, turned his attention to pistols. His first design appeared in prototype form in 1894 and was test fired at the Colt factory in July 1895. The first Browning model to enter production, however, did so at Fabrique National in Belgium in 1899.

The French Le Mat of 1856 held 9 rounds in an attempt to increase the handgun's firepower but resulted in an ugly and ungainly weapon. Browning's automatic design was to offer the shooter more ammunition in a compact package.

First steps

The first of the Browning prototypes was the .38 caliber semi-automatic pistol, which used a similar "flapper" system to his early machine guns (see Chapter 5). The gas vent was positioned approximately 2 inches from the muzzle and led the gasses upwards to strike a lever, which moved radially upwards and rearwards towards the

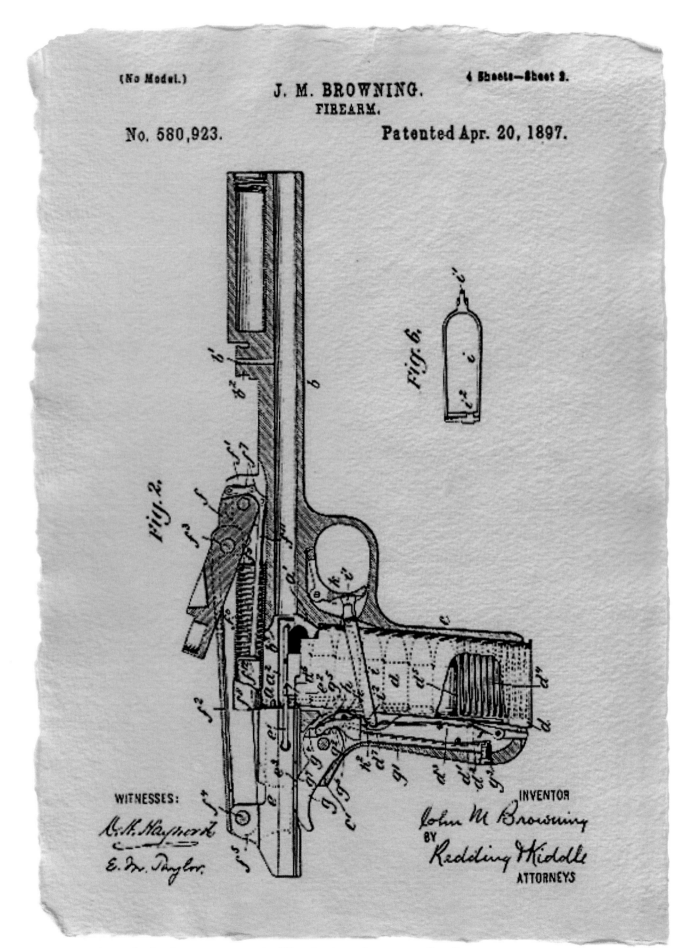

J. M. BROWNING.
FIREARM.

No. 580,923. Patented Apr. 20, 1897.

Fig. 6.

Fig. 2.

WITNESSES:

INVENTOR
John M Browning
BY
Redding & Kiddle
ATTORNEYS

Browning's design for his first gas-operated self-loader from the Patent office files.
The gun never actually went into production.

Left: A receipt for the payment made by FN to the Browning brothers for the first "Model 1900" Automatic Pistol.

Above: John M. Browning with a group of FN officials in 1910. The inventor is easily distinguished by his height and his Panama hat.

firer. The lever was linked to the breech bolt, which it drove to the rear, extracting and ejecting the used cartridge as it went, cocking the hammer and compressing the spring. When the rearward movement was completed the spring drove the bolt forward again, extracting a round from the magazine and chambering it, ready for the firer to pull the trigger and commence the next cycle. It was a neat design, just 8.5 inches long and weighing 36 ounces. A U.S. patent was obtained (580,923/1897) and the pistol was tested by Colt, who then bought U.S. manufacturing and marketing rights, although it was never put into production. The main disadvantage was the flapping lever, which obscured the firer's sight-line with every shot.

It's worth noting here that many of Browning's semi-automatics appeared in prototype form only and were never given individual names. To identify these in this

Colt Model 1900

I N THE LATTER PART of the 19th century the U.S. handgun scene was dominated by the revolver, although Colt was the first among U.S. weapons companies to appreciate the importance of the automatic pistol.

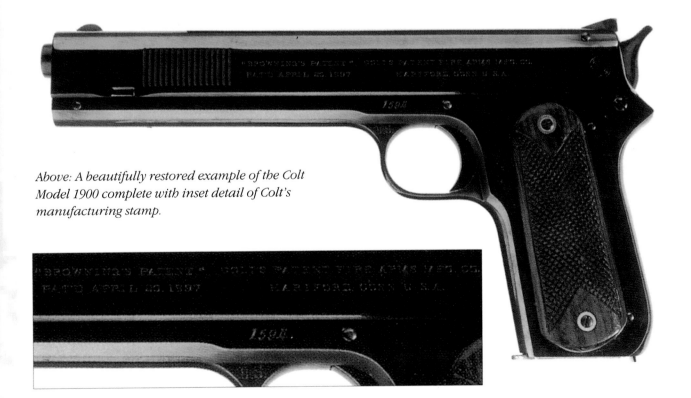

As in all aspects of the weapons industry, the crucial factor was to gain a military contract and with this aim in view, Colt set about developing a reliable and effective pistol for the U.S. Army and Navy. The first fruit of this was the M1898 and this was quickly developed into the M1900, chambered for the .38 ACP cartridge, and which had exceptionally functional lines as shown in this beautifully restored example.

Above: The prototype [U.S. Patent 580,924] which became the Model 1900 Colt automatic pistol.

Above: A beautifully restored example of the Colt Model 1900 complete with inset detail of Colt's manufacturing stamp.

book, the U.S. patent number is given plus the year in which it was allocated; e.g., 580,924/1897. There was usually a delay of about six months between Browning/Colt applying for a patent and the actual allocation of one.

Browning always strove for simplicity and appears to have concluded that a piston was an unnecessary complication in a handgun. He quickly turned to blowback operation in his next model, the .32 caliber semi-automatic pistol, (U.S. Patent 580,296/1897), which was completed in late 1895 and demonstrated to Colt in January 1896. In this weapon the gasses generated both propelled the bullet forwards and drove the empty cartridge case, together with the bolt to which it was secured, to the rear. As the bolt moved, the cartridge case was ejected and the action cocked, whereupon the spring, which was located above the barrel, drove it forward again. As with Browning's previous submission to the company, Colt bought the manufacturing rights to the gun but never put it into production.

Next came two versions of a .38 caliber semi-automatic (U.S. Patents 590,924/1897 and 708,794/1902) which introduced positive locking of the barrel and slide to ensure a secure seal at the breach when firing. Both employed top ejection when built, but were later modified to the more sensible side ejection. Once again, Colt tested both and then bought the sales rights, but never placed either in production.

Colt also bought sales rights to a different design, also in .38 caliber (U.S. Patent 580,925/1897). This was totally different in appearance to any other Browning semi-automatic, with a cylindrical slide and frame, the spring being wrapped around the barrel. Although very neat in appearance and performing well in tests this, too, was not proceeded with.

Colt Model 1900

The Colt Model 1900 (U.S. Patent 580,924/1897) was John Browning's first semi-automatic pistol design to be placed in production in the United States; indeed, it was the first semi-automatic of *any* design to be produced in the U.S. He completed the design and demonstrated it to Colt in 1896; it was accepted by them in 1898 and marketed from February 1900 onwards. This pistol used the short-recoil system and was the first to have the characteristic Browning appearance of a long rectangular main body containing the barrel and action, a square-cut butt almost at right angles, and with a trigger guard bridging the angle between the two. Chambered for the .38 ACP (Automatic Colt Pistol) cartridge specially designed for automatic pistols, the Model 1900 was 9 inches long, weighed 2 pounds 3 ounces, and in the earliest production versions the rear sight also served as the safety, locking the hammer when pushed down.

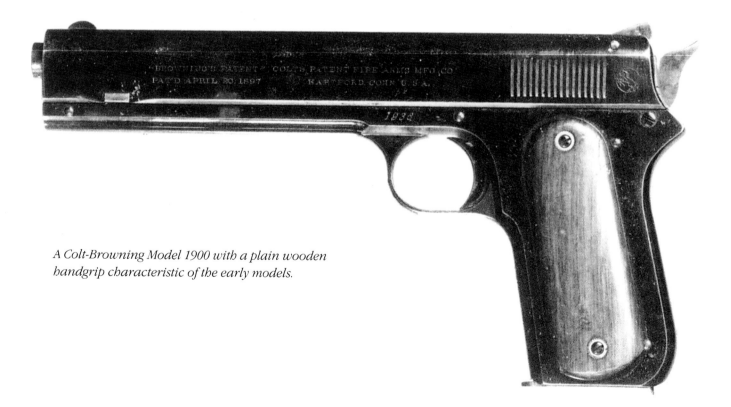

A Colt-Browning Model 1900 with a plain wooden handgrip characteristic of the early models.

Above: The Colt Model 1902 Sporting Pistol which featured a shortened firing pin and molded rubber grips.

Above: Inset detail of the patent and manufacturer stamps including the rimless and smokeless designations.

There were three models. The original was designated the Sporting and entered production in 1900. In 1902 it was modified to have an adjustable (as opposed to fixed) rear sight, a shorter firing-pin and abbreviated hammer; production ended in 1908. The Military, introduced in 1902, had an eight (as opposed to seven) round magazine, a larger grip and a slide stop, while the Pocket was identical to the Sporting apart from having a shorter barrel. Production of the Pocket ended in 1927 and of the Military the following year. Total production of all three types was approximately 112,000.

FN Model 1900 .32 caliber Pistol

The Fabrique Nationale Model 1900 became the first of Browning's designs to be sold to a foreign company, and testing of it was completed by him after he had finished working on the Colt Model 1900. Fabrique Nationale of Liége, Belgium, acquired the rights to produce and market it outside the United States in 1897 and production pistols began leaving the Belgian factory in late 1899. It was a major success. Chambered for the .32 ACP round, its design had a blowback action very similar to that of his

earlier 1895 .32 caliber weapon, but with numerous refinements. It was also very small in size, with an overall length of 6.75 inches and a weight of 1 pound 6 ounces. The magazine, which was housed in the butt, held seven rounds. This FN Model 1900 remained in production until 1910, by which time some 725,000 had been sold. One particular example achieved an unparalleled degree of notoriety, having been used by Gavrilo Princip to assassinate Archduke Franz Ferdinand of Austria-Hungary in Sarajevo, June 28, 1914, the event which triggered World War I.

Above: The prototype of the 7.65 mm Modele 1899/1900 FN pistol.

Above: FN model 1900 7.65 mm pistol engraved with gold inlay.

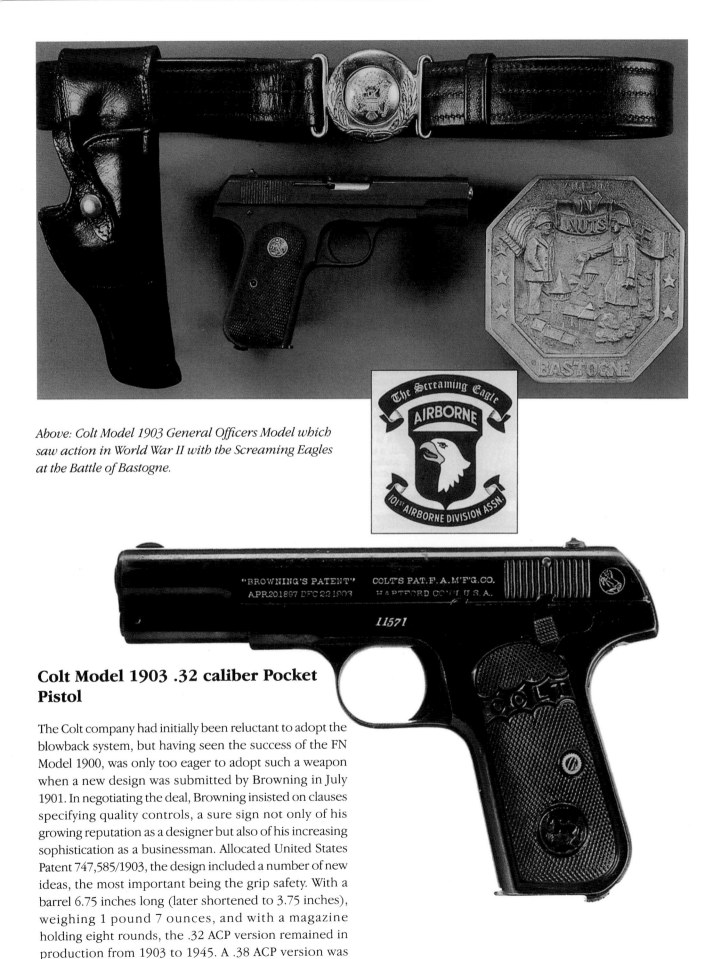

Above: Colt Model 1903 General Officers Model which saw action in World War II with the Screaming Eagles at the Battle of Bastogne.

Colt Model 1903 .32 caliber Pocket Pistol

The Colt company had initially been reluctant to adopt the blowback system, but having seen the success of the FN Model 1900, was only too eager to adopt such a weapon when a new design was submitted by Browning in July 1901. In negotiating the deal, Browning insisted on clauses specifying quality controls, a sure sign not only of his growing reputation as a designer but also of his increasing sophistication as a businessman. Allocated United States Patent 747,585/1903, the design included a number of new ideas, the most important being the grip safety. With a barrel 6.75 inches long (later shortened to 3.75 inches), weighing 1 pound 7 ounces, and with a magazine holding eight rounds, the .32 ACP version remained in production from 1903 to 1945. A .38 ACP version was introduced in 1908 and remained in production until 1946. A total of 710,224 of both types were produced.

Above: Another example of the Model 1903 with different grip markings.

Above: The Colt Model 1908 .38 Pocket Pistol issued to Brigadier-General George C. McDonald of the U.S. Army Air Force with memorabilia photos. His Colt sidearm was a treasured weapon.

Left : An example of the diminutive Colt Model 1908 Hammerless .25 Pocket Pistol which was intended as a concealable personal defense weapon.

The Model 1908 came in many guises all based on Browning's original design and produced exclusively by FN until Colt bought U.S. rights.

*Above: Browning's Prototype for
the 9 mm FN Modele 1903 seen
from both sides.*

Below: Cut-away view of the same gun.

Right: "Large Model" 9 mm pistol being fired from the shoulder with a holster-butt.

Above: An original FN-made example.

FN Model 1903 9 mm Pistol

Concurrently with the Colt Model 1903, John Browning also developed a new weapon at the request of the management at Fabrique Nationale, which became the FN Model 1903 9 mm Pistol (its European designation was *Modèle 1903 Pistolet Automatique Grande Modèle*). This had many similarities to the Colt Model 1903 but fired the 9 mm Browning Long, a 9 x 20 mm cartridge specially developed for this weapon. The pistol had a 5-inch barrel with the recoil spring located underneath, and a seven-round magazine. At 8 inches in length it weighed 2 pounds.

FN Model 1906 6.35 mm Vest Pocket Semi-Automatic Pistol
alongside a banknote showing its compact design.

A new feature was the hold-open device, which stopped the action to the rear once the last round had been fired. It not only told the firer that the magazine was empty, but held the action to the rear so that, after changing the magazine, all the user needed to do was push the action forward to continue firing with the minimum of delay.

Optional extras included a longer ten-round magazine and a detachable shoulder stock, which could also serve as a holster. This weapon was intended for the military market, although many armies continued to be very wary of blowback operation with military calibers. Some 153,000 were eventually produced by Fabrique

Nationale in Belgium and Husqvarna in Sweden, with sales being made to armies in Belgium, the Netherlands, Paraguay, Sweden and Imperial Russia. Huge numbers of unauthorized copies were also made, particularly in Spain.

FN Model 1906 6.35 mm Vest Pocket Semi-Automatic Pistol

Essentially a smaller version of the FN Model 1903, the FN 6.35 mm Vest Pocket Semi-Automatic Pistol was designed by John Browning in 1905 and entered production in Belgium in the same year. Production

These examples of the Colt version of the tiny FN 6.35 mm Vest Pocket pistol are just 4.5 inches long.

continued until the occupying Germans stopped non-military work in 1940, but manufacture restarted after the war, this time in .25 caliber. Colt obtained the U.S. license from John Browning in 1908 and produced the pistol in .25 caliber until 1917. Just 4.5 inches long and weighing 13 ounces, the original Vest Pocket pistol had a magazine holding six rounds and was unusual for a John Browning design in being hammerless. In the post-war versions the weight was reduced to 10 ounces and length to 4 inches. Many millions of this weapon have been produced; well over one million by FN, approximately half a million by Colt and an estimated 2 million-plus clones by other makers, mainly in Spain.

FN Models 1910 and 1922

John M. Browning designed this blowback-operated, semi-automatic pistol in 1909–10 and it was immediately accepted for testing and manufacture by Fabrique Nationale as a replacement for the Model 1900. The Model 1910 differed from his earlier designs by having the recoil spring wrapped around the barrel, and was chambered for either of two rounds which Browning himself had designed: the .32 ACP (7.65 x17 mm) and .38 ACP (9 x 17 mm). It was in production from 1910 to 1954, during which time over 500,000 were manufactured, being particularly popular with police forces. In the early 1920s Browning made slight modifications to the design to meet a requirement of the newly-created Yugoslavian Army and this entered production as the Model 1922; it was in the same calibers but had a slightly longer barrel and an extended grip which enabled magazine capacity to be increased from seven to nine rounds (.32 ACP) or from six to eight rounds (.38 ACP). Over 400,000 had been made by the time production ended in 1983.

Above: A Model 10/71 which was a second production run of the 1910 Model in the 1970s.

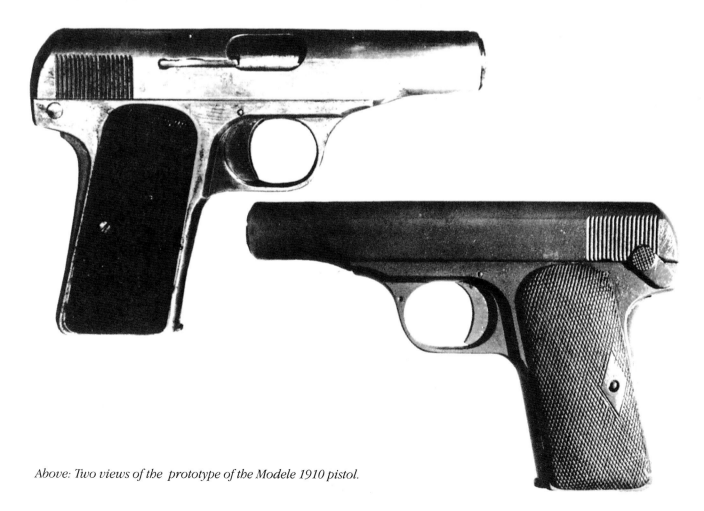

Above: Two views of the prototype of the Modele 1910 pistol.

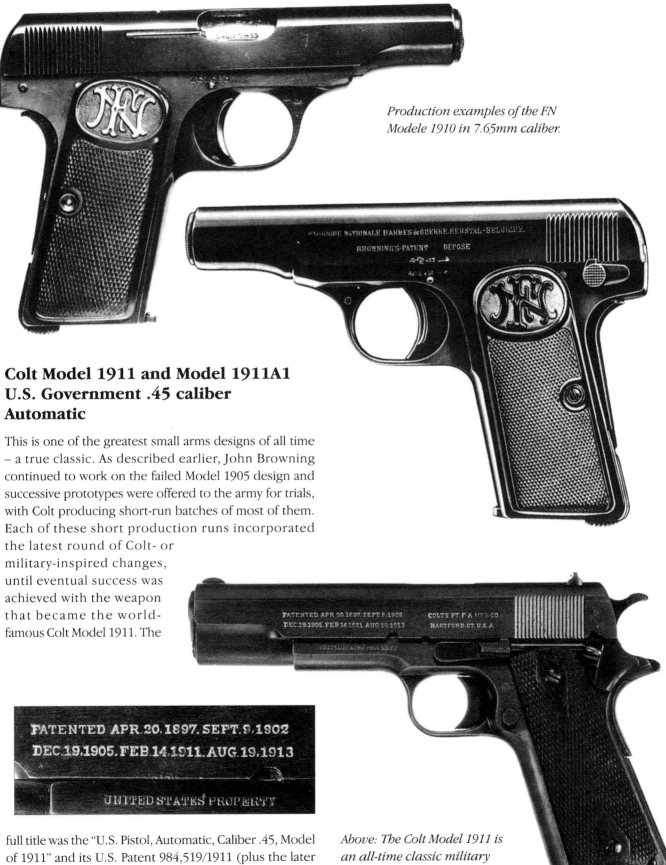

Production examples of the FN Modele 1910 in 7.65mm caliber.

Colt Model 1911 and Model 1911A1 U.S. Government .45 caliber Automatic

This is one of the greatest small arms designs of all time – a true classic. As described earlier, John Browning continued to work on the failed Model 1905 design and successive prototypes were offered to the army for trials, with Colt producing short-run batches of most of them. Each of these short production runs incorporated the latest round of Colt- or military-inspired changes, until eventual success was achieved with the weapon that became the world-famous Colt Model 1911. The

full title was the "U.S. Pistol, Automatic, Caliber .45, Model of 1911" and its U.S. Patent 984,519/1911 (plus the later 1,070,582/1913 for the mechanical safety). The first delivery of the very first batch of military models was made on January 4, 1912 at a cost to the government of $14.25 for each pistol and one magazine. Production of the Commercial Government Model for the civil market also

Above: The Colt Model 1911 is an all-time classic military handgun.

Two examples of the M1911A1: one with fixed back sight and lightened trigger and another with an adjustable back sight.

started in 1912, this weapon differing only in a higher standard of finish, the markings and a different range of serial numbers, all prefixed by the letter "C."

Firing the newly developed .45 ACP round, the original production weapon was 8.5 inches long, with a 3.75-inch (later extended to 5-inch) barrel and weighed 2 pounds 7 ounces. There were fixed sights on the slide, which also had serrations on either side to help the shooter grip it for cocking. There were no less than three safeties: thumb-operated manual, the grip (a John Browning patent), and a magazine safety.

Up to the outbreak of World War I, some 100,000 Model 1911s had been delivered to the U.S. Army, Navy and Marine Corps, but these were nowhere near sufficient

M1911 with the rare Tansley loaded-weapon indicator. This was a mechanism designed to alert the shooter to the presence of a round in the chamber. It never went into production.

for wartime needs, so in 1917–18 nine further factories were contracted to produce the Model 1911. In the event, only at Remington did any actually leave the production line, wartime production being: Colt – 488,850; Remington – 21,676.

In the early 1920s various improvements were discussed and some of them implemented in the Model 1911A1 which was approved in 1923. The changes were relatively minor, the visual alterations being a longer comb (hammer spur) and chamfering behind the trigger. The remaining changes, such as the dimensions of the lands in the barrel, were internal. Curiously, the only functional change, an improvement to the magazine retaining mechanism and implemented after some 3,000 had been

produced, was not marked by a change in model suffix.

Over the years the weapon appeared in three main calibers – the original .45, followed by .38 and then by .22, all of them in various grades of finish – while a special barrel and magazine were produced in .455 caliber to meet British World War I orders.

The M1911A1 was the model produced during World War II, albeit with some minor changes to facilitate mass production. Some 2,300,000 were produced in total, the approximate split between manufacturers being: Colt – 17 percent, Ithaca Gun Company – 20 percent, Remington Rand – 41 percent, and Union Switch & Signal Company – 22 percent.

Production of the Model 1911A1 was phased out by

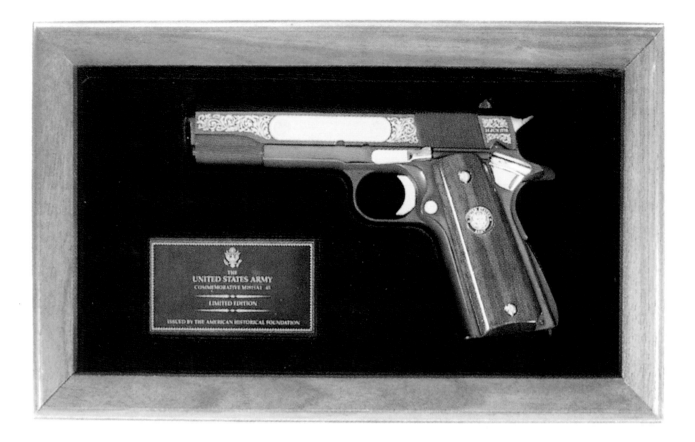

Colt in favor of the Series 70 Government Model, manufactured from 1971 to 1983, which had various minor improvements, and this was followed by the Series 80 Government Model in 1983, which incorporated an additional firing-pin safety lock and a redesigned half-cock notch.

In the 1970s it became clear that the U.S. military needed a new combat pistol. Production of the M1911A1 had ceased many years previously, the existing in-service stock was wearing out and there were ever-decreasing supplies in the warehouses. There was a very strong lobby to simply place the M1911A1 back in production, albeit updated to make maximum use of modern production methods. Despite the strength of feeling the Pentagon started a new project, based on a requirement for a double-action weapon chambered for the NATO standard 9 mm Parabellum round, in which an updated M1911A1 failed by a very narrow margin to win over an Italian design from Beretta, which, on January 14, 1985 was adopted as the "Pistol, Automatic, Caliber 9 mm, M9." The arguments still rumble on, but while the M9 has proved to be successful it is nevertheless true that for the M1911/M1911A1 to have remained in front-line service with the U.S. armed forces for well over seven decades with such very minor changes is strong testimony to the essential rightness of the original design.

A number of versions have appeared chambered for the smaller .380 ACP round, and many users, such as police and security guards, preferred something less powerful than the .45, which was intended to kill a charging enemy at very close range. All such versions shared the general appearance of the M1911, together with many of the components, although the barrel and chamber were obviously smaller, while the magazine held nine rounds as opposed to seven of .45 caliber. First of these was the Super .38 1929 Model, which was followed by the Super Match .38 1935 Model. The latter sold only in small numbers on the civilian market, but in 1939 the British, desperate for any weapons they could lay their hands on bought some 1,200 for their armed forces. A total of 163,100 were produced.

The .380 Mustang, introduced in 1983, had a shorter barrel and butt, combined with a smaller frame, reducing overall length to 5.5 inches and magazine capacity to five rounds. It was supplemented in 1987 by the .380 Mustang Pocketlite with an aluminum frame, which reduced the weight from 18.5 to 12.5 ounces, albeit at the cost of increased recoil. In 1990 the .380 Mustang II appeared, which combined the Mustang slide and barrel with the larger .380 Government Model frame, and restoring the number of rounds in the magazine back to seven.

Target shooters have always liked the M1911 and from the early days have modified and adjusted their pistols in order to enhance the accuracy. Observing this, Colt have produced a variety of more accurate versions using the highest grade components and special sights to meet this market need. The first was the .45 National Match in 1933, which was based on the M1911, while a

Commemorative examples of the M1911 which date from World War I.

Above: A beautifully engraved example of a M1911A1 done by master engraver Alvin A. White.

combined with a shorter slide (which was still made of steel) and a shorter barrel, all of which brought the weight down to just under 26 ounces. This weapon was also made chambered for the 9 mm Parabellum, .38 Super and 7.65 mm Parabellum rounds. Some users found the Commander's aluminum alloy frame less than satisfactory, so a steel-framed version, known as the Combat Commander, was introduced in 1971 which brought the weight up to 33 ounces.

Another target-shooting version was the Combat Elite model, in .45 caliber and retaining the main elements of the standard M1911A1, but with a stainless steel frame, triple-dot sights, streamlined magazine aperture for quicker loading, larger ejection port, grip safety, and wrap-around rubber handgrips.

Gold Cup National Match version of the M1911A1 was produced in 1957.

The M1911A1 Commander was developed by Colt in 1949 as a lighter and handier version. Still chambered for the .45 ACP round, it had an aluminum alloy frame,

The M1911A1 was made by four major suppliers. This exceptional example was made by the Union Switch and Signal Company.

U.S. & S. CO.
SWISSVALE, PA. U.S.A.

The 10 mm Auto Pistol cartridge was introduced in the mid-1980s and has had a mixed reception. It is undoubtedly powerful but has a substantial recoil, making it too powerful for many shooters to control properly, especially in combat scenarios. One response to this

Both sides of a Remington-made M1911A1. The company produced 949,000 units, some way behind Colt's 1.8 million production total.

problem has been the development of a 10 mm Lite round with a reduced load. Colt developed the Delta Elite model in 1987, which was essentially an M1911A1 rechambered for the 10 mm round, and with special markings including a delta sign on the butt.

The Colt Double Eagle is also based closely on the M1911A1, but has a double-action trigger with a decocking lever. It also has wrap-around handgrips, satin finish and other minor enhancements.

General Officers in the U.S. armed forces carry pistols when necessary although they would only need to use them as a very last resort, and want a weapon which will not interfere with carrying out their other duties. To meet this need the Rock Island Arsenal developed the General Officers' Model, which is essentially an M1911A1 with a shorter (7.25-inch) barrel, a six-round magazine, weight reduced from 39 to 34 ounces and a plate on the butt on which the general's name is engraved prior to issue. The Rock Island weapon was for military use only,

Above: The Colt Mk IV Series Government Model in bright finish.

Below: An M1911A1 Ithaca-made U.S. Eighth Air Force issue pistol with holsters and magazine pouch.

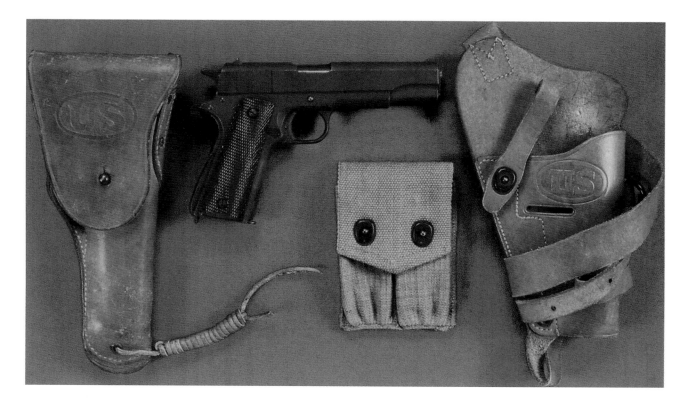

The M1911 pistol in .22 caliber.

and at the end of their service the recipients could either return it or purchase it at a nominal price. Colt developed a similar weapon for sale on the civilian market.

.22 Long Rifle caliber Training Pistol

There are obvious benefits in having a training weapon which can simulate the appearance, weight, operating characteristics and feel of a full-size weapon, but in a smaller caliber. Thus, at the request of the U.S. Army, John Browning started work in about 1913 to develop a derivative of the M1911 chambered for the .22 Long Rifle

Eight Air Force issue Union Switch and Signal Company M1911A1 with shoulder holster owned by Captain Arthur C. Stipe, and known to have been carried on active missions over Europe during WWII. [See inset picture]

Despite strong opposition from supporters of the M1911A1 the Beretta 92F was adopted as the standard NATO pistol in 1985 in place of the gun that had served faithfully for over 7 decades.

Right: The Colt Mustang 380 which was introduced in 1983 still shows the heritage of its larger uncle – the M1911.

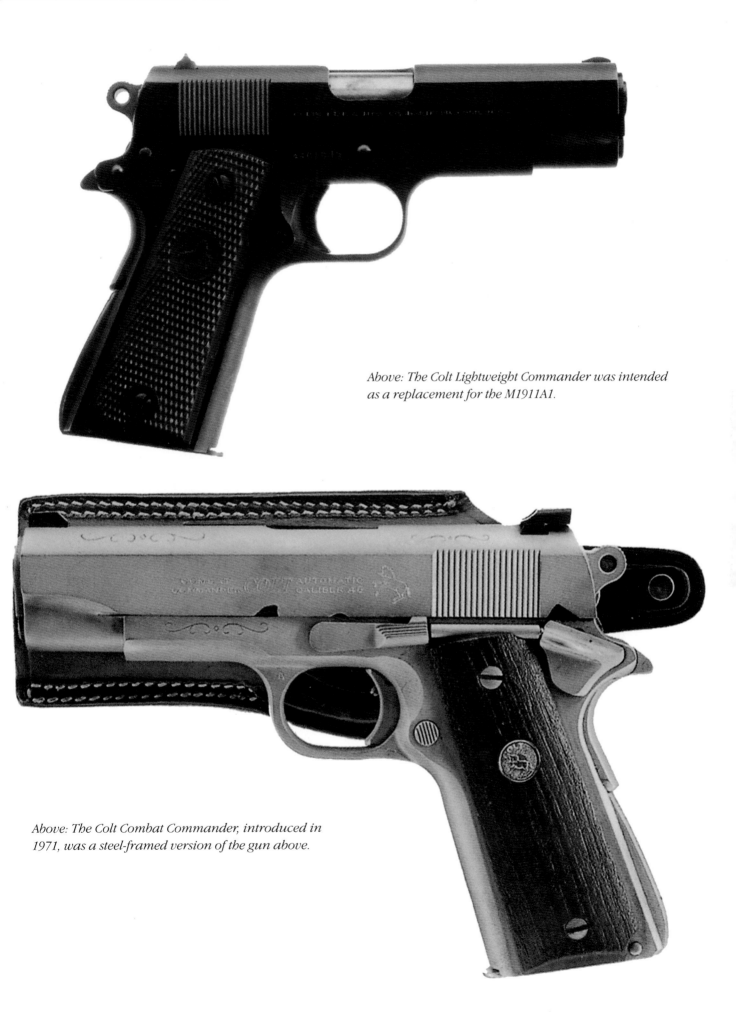

Above: The Colt Lightweight Commander was intended as a replacement for the M1911A1.

Above: The Colt Combat Commander, introduced in 1971, was a steel-framed version of the gun above.

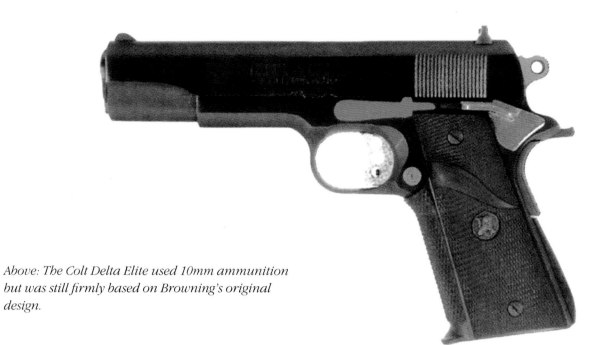

Above: The Colt Delta Elite used 10mm ammunition but was still firmly based on Browning's original design.

round and, with his usual expedition, prototypes were produced in 1915. This weapon was some 9 inches long, with a 4.25-inch barrel, and weighed approximately 1.5 pounds. As far as is known the prototypes were tested, but on the United States entering World War I in 1917 further work ceased for the duration, although John Browning incorporated some of the design features into the Woodsman while Colt resurrected the idea of a training pistol in 1931 (see below for both).

Left: Colt Double Eagle Combat Commander Pistol in classic .45 caliber with the motif on the shipping box "The Legend Lives" referring to its forefather the M1911.

Left: A boxed example of the Delta Elite. The red triangle in the black neoprene handgrip warns the shooter of the 10mm ammunition requirement.

Colt Ace

As described earlier, work on the .22 training pistol version of the M1911 stopped in 1917. The project was, however resurrected in the early 1920s and dragged on until 1927, when the U.S. Army decided that the plan for a .22 version of the standard service pistol was impractical and withdrew. In 1930, however, Colt ran a public consultation to see if there was any interest in such a weapon and, having received a positive response, they finished

A Colt Ace pistol made in 1939 designed as a training pistol in .22 caliber with detail of manufacturers markings.

development and then produced some 11,000 Ace pistols between 1931 and 1941. The one shortcoming of the Ace as a training tool was that the recoil was not as marked as that of the full-size weapon, so a new version, the .22 Super Ace, was introduced in 1937 with a floating chamber which served to magnify the kick from the .22 round to virtually the same as that of the .45 round. Some 13,800 were made between 1937 and 1945, most of them going to the U.S. Army, who thus finally received the small caliber service "look-alike" they had asked for no less than quarter of a century earlier.

There was a rather curious postscript in that in 1938 Colt started to market a conversion kit, so that owners of normal .45 M1911s could adapt them to fire .22 ammunition. This kit involved a special slide, .22 barrel (with the floating chamber), recoil spring and other minor parts, together with a ten-round magazine. As if this was not enough, Colt also produced another conversion unit which could be used by owners of the .22 Service Model Ace to adapt it to fire .45 ammunition.

series: the first, or pre-Woodsman series covers weapons manufactured between 1915 and 1927, of which some 54,000 were manufactured. This was followed by the three Woodsman series, which reflect the changes in frame adopted by the company. Series 1 was made in 1927–47; Series 2 in 1947–55; and Series 3 1955–77. There was only one grade of pre-Woodsman, but once it was re-designated Woodsman, Colt produced the weapons in three grades: Sport (introduced in 1933), Target, which was basically the Sport with a longer barrel, and the Match Target (introduced in 1938), with heavier barrel and better sights. In addition, during the post-World War II period only, there were three less expensive versions: Challenger (1950–55), Huntsman (1955–77) and Targetsman (1959–1977). Wartime production (1942–45) was confined to the Woodsman Match Target and was almost entirely for the U.S. Government.

Barrels were either 4.5 or 6.5 inches long and the action was blowback in semi-automatic mode only. The weapons weighed 1 pounds 12 ounces (6-inch barrel) or

Colt Woodsman .22 caliber Automatic Pistol

While working on the training pistol for the U.S. Government John M. Browning also designed a .22 caliber training pistol for civilian use. Production started at the Colt factory in 1915 under the designation .22 Automatic Target Pistol although Browning did not obtain a patent until three years later (1,276,716/1918). Since the weapon was intended for civilian use, Browning was not constrained by the demands of the U.S. Government and was able to dispense with the hammer, so beloved of the U.S. Cavalry, while the slide was comparatively short and did not cover the barrel.

The weapon was an immediate success and remained in production, in various forms, from 1915 until 1977. It had originally been intended as a target and training pistol, but its capabilities were quickly appreciated by outdoorsmen, such as hunters and trappers; indeed, it achieved such popularity that Colt changed its name to the Woodsman in 1927. Experts divide the type into four

The Colt Pre-Woodsman model was produced between 1915 and 1927 when it was officially named the Woodsman.

1 pound 10 ounces (4.5-inch barrel). There was a thumb-operated manual safety on the left side of the weapon, and an automatic safety where the pistol could only be fired if the breechblock was fully forward.

Above: First we show a Series 1 Woodsman with standard markings and features, including a 6.5 inch barrel, walnut grips and the magazine catch on the heel of the butt.

Above: Next is a Series 2 Woodsman made in 1954, which has been further modified by addition of wrap-around grips.

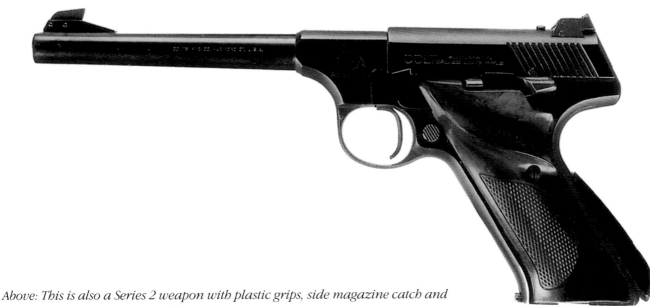

Above: This is also a Series 2 weapon with plastic grips, side magazine catch and a plastic adapter at the rear of the grip.

A Series 2 Match Target Pistol

A Match Target version made from a pre-war Series 1 fitted with an adjustable rear sight and special extended grips which attracted the name "Elephant Ears."

An elaborate Series 3 version with heavier barrel and the magazine catch moved back to the heel of the butt.

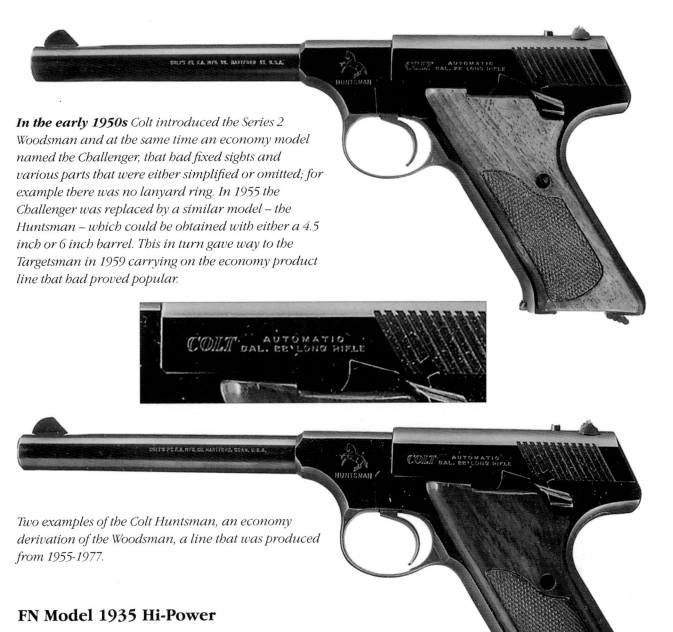

In the early 1950s Colt introduced the Series 2 Woodsman and at the same time an economy model named the Challenger, that had fixed sights and various parts that were either simplified or omitted; for example there was no lanyard ring. In 1955 the Challenger was replaced by a similar model – the Huntsman – which could be obtained with either a 4.5 inch or 6 inch barrel. This in turn gave way to the Targetsman in 1959 carrying on the economy product line that had proved popular.

Two examples of the Colt Huntsman, an economy derivation of the Woodsman, a line that was produced from 1955-1977.

FN Model 1935 Hi-Power

This famous and widely-used pistol is known by a number of names, including Model 1935, P-35, Hi-Power and Grand Puissance. It was the last automatic pistol to be designed by John M. Browning, who started work on it very soon after the end of World War I. It is not clear whether this was in response to a French enquiry for a semi-automatic pistol chambered for the French 9 mm Longue round and with a fifteen-round magazine, or whether Browning simply revisited the M1911 design with a view to improving on it. Whatever the reason, in early 1921, Browning produced two slightly different designs, tested the prototypes and then sent them to Colt who prepared and submitted the U.S. patent application. Colt was not interested in manufacturing the design, however, so Browning then sent it to Fabrique Nationale, where, having selected one of the two for further work, the company built two more prototypes which were submitted to the French army for trials in 1922. The comments of the French army were then studied and a new model was produced for trials in 1923, which it passed

with flying colors.

John Browning's patent for this pistol took a considerable time to process and the number 1,618,510/1927 was only finally allocated in February 1927, a few months after he had died in Belgium.

Browning's death resulted in the work on the new pistol being taken over by his friend and colleague at Fabrique Nationale, the Belgian, Dieudonné Saive, and development proceeded slowly. This slowness was caused in part by a general reluctance among most armies to buy new pistols – there were vast stocks of World War I weapons on hand – and the general economic climate, which was, to say the least, bad and getting worse. The

The Browning Hi-Power was manufactured from 1935 onwards. This is a Sport Model made for the civilian market.

new design was finally completed in 1929 and was now chambered for the 9 mm Parabellum round with a magazine containing thirteen rounds in a double-row layout. No orders were received for a further five years, however, until it was finally placed into production for the Belgian army as the Model 1935. As is usual with new weapons, once the home army had placed an order, others quickly followed from countries as far apart as China, Estonia, Latvia, Lithuania Peru and Romania.

The Model 1935 is chambered for either the 9 mm Parabellum or 9 mm Luger rounds of which the detachable box magazine holds thirteen, plus one in the chamber. The weapon operates on the short-recoil principle, with the breechblock locked temporarily to the slide as the weapon is fired and they recoil together until the bullet leaves the muzzle, whereupon the rear end of the barrel is tilted downwards by lugs following a predetermined path, which disengages it from the slide and breechblock. The latter components then continue rearwards, carrying the empty case with them until it is deflected by the ejector and expelled to the right. When the breechblock hits the buffer, it and the slide are then pushed forward by the return spring, picking up a new round as they pass over the magazine and chambering it. The only criticism of the design concerns the trigger mechanism, which is generally considered not to be as good as in the M1911.

The Model 1935 was adopted first by the Belgian Army and then by many other armed forces. Inevitably a weapon which has been in production for so many years and which has been used by so many armed forces has undergone many minor modifications. Pre-war variants included fixed or adjustable sights and a removable wooden stock.

The Model 1935 had a mixed history during World War II. When the Germans invaded Belgium in 1940, Fabrique Nationale with its considerable design and production facilities was one of their early targets. The staff were largely uncooperative and many of the designers and engineers escaped to England, but the home factory, now under German control and renamed DWM Lüttich (the German name for Liege), continued to produce the Model 1935 Hi-Power under the German designation Pistole Modell 640(b). The quality of workmanship was very variable and it is believed that some 300,000 were produced.

When the FN staff arrived in London they attempted to reverse engineer some pre-war specimens of the Model 1935 but as far as is known, no production took place in the United Kingdom. Inglis of Canada, a former engineering works, set up a production line in Toronto, manufacturing some 150,000 in 1944–45. Most of these went to the Nationalist Chinese army, although small numbers were also supplied to the British, Canadian and Greek armies, as well.

The Germans demolished as much as they could of the

An example of a WWII production gun from Herstal – note the rough finish of this gun. Wartime production of the gun was designated as the Pistole Modell 640[b] during the German occupation of Belgium.

factory before abandoning it in the face of the Allied advance and then added to the destruction by bombarding it with V-2 rockets. Despite this, the Fabrique Nationale staff soon had the Hi-Power back in production under the new designation, Model 1946, but whatever FN might call it, it remains the Model 1935 to the rest of the world. It sold well and was adopted by many armies, including the British, who used it to replace a mixed bag of Smith & Wesson and Webley revolvers, Inglis-made Model 1935s and other sidearms. Fabrique Nationale produced a Hi-Power Mark 2 in the 1970s, which had an ambidextrous safety catch, better-shaped handgrips, wider sights and a phosphated finish. It was not a success and was dropped in 1987, to be replaced in 1989 by the Hi-Power Mark 3 which had slightly more radical improvements, including an enlarged ejection port, new hand grips, and the back sight dovetailed into a mount to facilitate changing. The standard Mark 3 was intended for military use, and the Mark 3S for police and civil use.

The original production version of the Model 1935 is chambered for the 9 x 19 mm Parabellum round and is 7.8 inches long with a 4.75-inch barrel. It weighs 2 pounds 3 ounces and has a muzzle velocity of 1,150 ft/sec. The Hi-Power Mark 3 is very similar, but marginally lighter.

Colt after 1970

Because of the inherent excellence of John Browning's design, the Model 1911 and its successor the Model 1911A1 are among the most modified handguns ever made. Colt alone has produced well over fifty variants, and many more have been produced outside the United States.

Production of the Model 1911A1 continued at Colt until 1971 when it was succeeded by the Mark IV Government Model Series 70, which had a marginally heavier slide and some minor internal changes, and was made in .45 ACP, .38 Super, 9 mm Parabellum and 9 mm Steyr calibers. There were Government (i.e., standard), Gold Cup National Match and Gunsite versions, as well as the Series 70 Service Model WWI, which was a straight reproduction of the original M1911. This was followed by the Mark IV Series 80, introduced in 1983, which had a minor change to the firing pin safety, then by a plethora of further variants in the 1990s and in the start of the 21st century.

FNH

Fabrique Nationale established a subsidiary company in the United States to market its produces, designated "FNH Inc." (i.e., Fabrique Nationale Herstal) and among its products are several modern versions of the Model 1935 Hi-Power. These include the Model HP-SA, Model HP-SA-SFS and Model HP-DA/HP-DA), which differ from each other mainly in whether the trigger is double- or single-

The FN-Browning Model 49 was introduced in 2000 and has a 16 round magazine for police use and a 10 round version for civilian purposes. It is chambered for either .40 S&W or 9 mm Parabellum ammunition.

action; all are chambered for the 9 mm Parabellum cartridge.

Browning Arms Company

The Browning Arms Company of Morgan, Utah, has continued the John M. Browning legacy with an extensive range of semi-automatic pistols based on the founder's designs. Following on from John M. Browning's intense interest in .22 caliber, the Browning Company markets the Buck Mark series of rimfire, blowback action, semi-automatic pistols in a wide variety of finishes and all chambered for the .22 Long Rifle cartridge. The centerfire range is based on the Fabrique Nationale Hi-Power, with models available for either 9 mm Luger or .40 S&W cartridges. The PRO-9 is a double-action pistol with a 4-inch barrel and a stainless steel slide, on a polymer frame. Higher up the range is the Hi-Power Mark III in an overall matte finish and then the Hi-Power Standard, which is almost identical with the Mark III but with a better finish. Top of the range is the Hi-Power Practical with a silver-chromed frame, blackened slide and Pachmayr grips.

Other manufacturers

Many other manufacturers continue to produce a vast range of weapons based on John M. Browning's pistol designs, particularly the M1911 whose copyright has expired.

Special editions

The Model 1911, 1911A1 and Hi-Power have all been manufactured as special editions to mark a particular anniversary. Engraved versions have also been offered for a

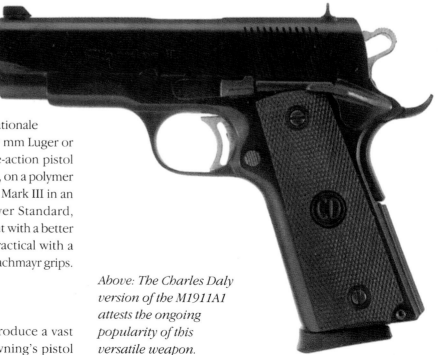

Above: The Charles Daly version of the M1911A1 attests the ongoing popularity of this versatile weapon.

The Capitan Model introduced in 1993 was a development of the Hi-Power Model.

limited period of time.

The Browning Company, for example, imported the 1970s Renaissance Hi-Power featuring heavy engraving, synthetic pearl grips and a gold-plated trigger, while the Louis XIV Model, imported in 1980–84, had different pattern engraving, leaf backsight and walnut grips. Yet another special edition was the Hi-Power Centennial Model of 1978 with a chrome-plated finish. Some special editions have also been chambered for different rounds such as the .30 Luger, .25 and .380.

Replicas and illegal copies

A replica firearm is one which is knowingly manufactured as a direct copy of an historic weapon and sold clearly labeled as such. This is usually perfectly legal and enables an enthusiast to obtain an exact copy of a weapon they admire, but where an original would be well beyond his or her pocket. John Browning's designs have been particular favorites in this area, particularly the greatly admired Model 1911, and Colt, for example, has produced such replicas.

What has always been illegal, however, is that for many centuries, unscrupulous arms dealers have manufactured and traded unauthorized copies of firearms, which have varied in quality from excellent to so bad that they represent a greater hazard to the user than to the target. Browning pistols have been manufactured under proper legal license in, for example, Argentina, Belgium, Brazil, Norway and Sweden, but both Browning and his properly authorized licensees, have suffered particularly badly from such piracy, partly because his designs were so good, but also because he strove always for simplicity and a minimum of parts, many of which were carefully conceived in order to fulfil more than one function.

The most usual method used to make such counterfeits is "reverse engineering," where a genuine example is dismantled down to the component level then every piece copied in the most minute detail. Sometimes this is done in order to sell such weapons to terrorists or others who want to use them in combat, but it is also done in order to fool unwary collectors who think that they have found a desirable weapon at considerably less than the usual price. In the case of Browning designs, unauthorized copies of virtually all his handguns have appeared over the years, the two main, but by no means the only, sources being the Eibar region of Spain and the North-West Frontier of India and Pakistan.

Buck Mark Pistols

BROWNING ADDED THIS .22 RIMFIRE PISTOL to their range to perhaps echo the Challenger/Huntsman ethos of the 1950s. A useful lightweight .22, chambered by hand for the Long Rifle Cartridge, that would appeal to outdoorsmen. Names like the Camper and Field reflect this. The action is a straight blow-back design, with a crisp single action trigger and an aircraft grade 7075 aluminum frame machined to exacting tolerances for lightness. The 16 click Pro-target rear sight provides an excellent range of adjustment for greater accuracy. On slected models a wrap-around Ultra-Grip RXT provides the latest in hand grip technology. The EIS [Ergonomic Interactive Surface] grooving puts the shooters hand in the same place on the grip for every shot allowing for instinctive and accurate shooting. Here are examples of the range.

Camper: A rugged matte-blued pistol with the accuracy benefits of a tapered bull barrel. Also available in rust-resistant satin nickel finish.

Field: A standard model with attractive traditional walnut grips. Full length scope mount.

Micro Nickel: All the features of the Buck Mark Standard but with a 4 inch bull barrel and contrasting nickel and black finishes. Also available with a 5¹/₂ inch standard barrel.

Target 5.5: 5¹/₂ inch barrel with Pro-Target adjustable sights and Cocabolo grips.

Target Stainless: Stainless-steel barrel with Rosewood grips.

Bullseye Target URX: 7¹/₄ inch barrel with Ultra-Grip RX ambidextrous grips.

Hunter: Features a heavy 7¹/₂ inch barrel, an integrated scope mount and a Truglo/Marbles front sight and Cocabolo target style grips.

Contour 5.5:5¹/₂ inch distinctive contoured barrel

CHAPTER THREE

Browning Rifles

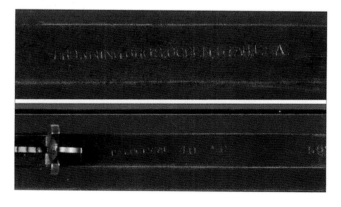

Above: Inset detail of the Rigby Ribs on each of the upper 3 flats of the octagonal top of the receiver named after John Rigby who first incorporated this design into his target rifles.

Above: Barrel marks clearly showing Browning Bros, Ogden, Utah, U.S.A., and the Patent number.

STANDARD PRODUCTION MODELS

Winchester/Browning Single-Shot Model 1885

John M. Browning's first major design was the Single-Shot Rifle whose dropping-block breech mechanism was granted U.S. Patent 220,271/1879. Production started at the Browning brothers' workshop in Ogden, Utah in 1880 after when the design was spotted by the Winchester Repeating Arms Company. This company bought the rights in 1883 and, having incorporated various minor changes, placed the weapon in production as the Winchester Single-Shot Model 1885. The Browning

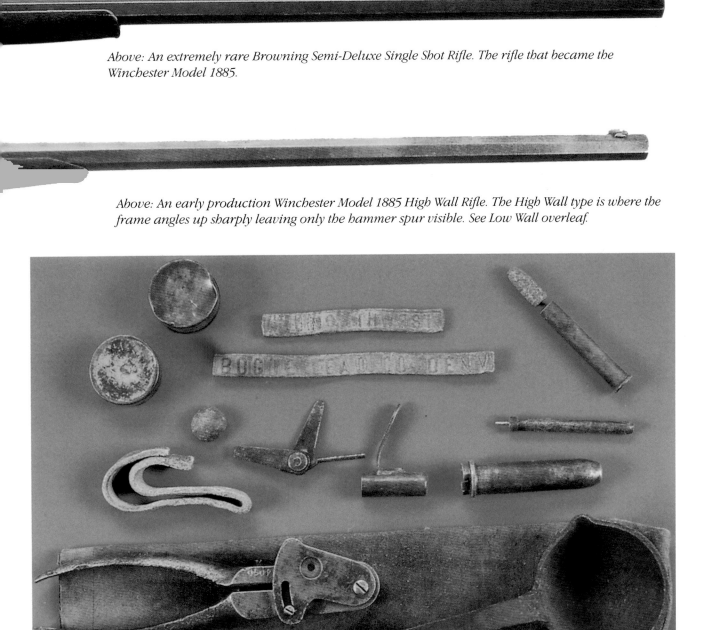

Above: An extremely rare Browning Semi-Deluxe Single Shot Rifle. The rifle that became the Winchester Model 1885.

Above: An early production Winchester Model 1885 High Wall Rifle. The High Wall type is where the frame angles up sharply leaving only the hammer spur visible. See Low Wall overleaf.

Above: The bullet mold that, legend has it, brought Browning and Winchester together. The mold was designed for the single-shot rifle and it came to the notice of one of the Winchester Sales agents and this alerted Oliver Winchester's son in law, Thomas Gray Bennett, then Vice President of Winchester to the existence of the single shot rifle. He was on the next train to Ogden where he secured the rights to manufacture the gun for Winchester.

Left: Barrel stamp from the early Winchester High Wall Rifle on the previous page. It shows that this gun was actually made by Browning and is possibly an example of the Browning brothers continuing to manufacture the guns even after they had sold the rights to Winchester.

brothers, being somewhat naïve in business matters at that early stage, were unaware that their own production was no longer permitted and continued to sell the rifle themselves until firmly instructed not to do so by the Winchester company, by which time some 600 examples had been made in their Ogden factory.

The Model 1885 was, like all of John M. Browning's designs, simple, straightforward and easy both to manufacture and to use. It had a lever action, a dropping block and an exposed hammer, which was cocked either automatically by closing the breechblock, or manually by hand. The hammer could also be set to the half-cock position as a safety measure. The breech was extremely compact and strong, and surprisingly sophisticated for such a young inventor at the very start of his distinguished career.

A wide variety of models were produced, such as the standard sporting version, a target and training rifle for the U.S. Army, and a carbine. The *Schützen* version, for the devotees of the German standing target firing discipline, had a heavier barrel, checkered pistol grip, nickeled butt-plate, palm rest beneath the fore-end and a vernier-type backsight fitted on the upper tang. There was also a wide variety of calibers – well over thirty by the time production ended – and ranging from .22 to .50. There was even a 20-gauge shotgun introduced in 1914, although it was made in only very small numbers and production ended within two years. Barrels ranged in length from 15 to 30 inches and overall weight from as little as 4 pounds 8 ounces to a massive 13 pounds for a *Schützen* model. The design also proved readily adaptable across the transition from black to smokeless powders.

It proved to be a great success and remained in production from 1885 to 1920, by which time some 140,000 had been manufactured. It has also been the subject of numerous special editions in the past 30 years.

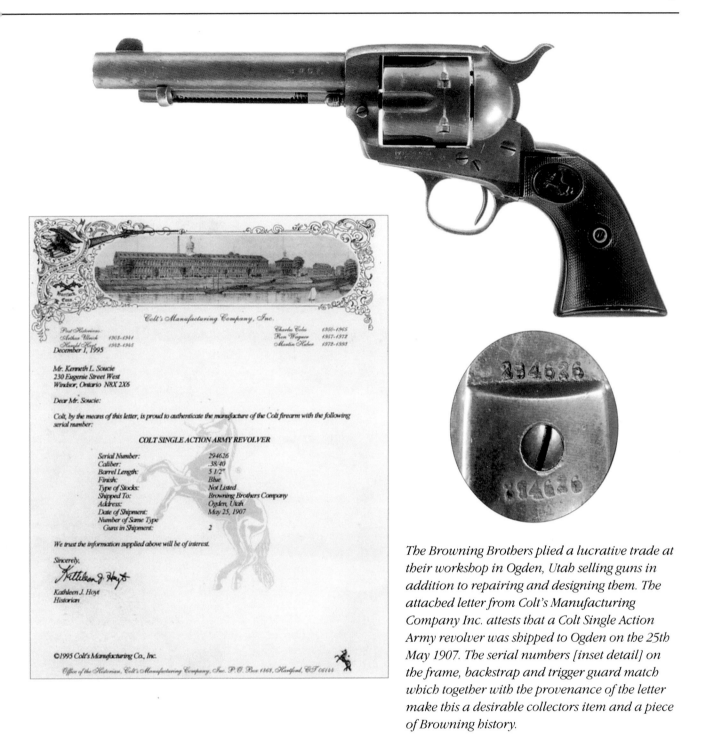

The Browning Brothers plied a lucrative trade at their workshop in Ogden, Utah selling guns in addition to repairing and designing them. The attached letter from Colt's Manufacturing Company Inc. attests that a Colt Single Action Army revolver was shipped to Ogden on the 25th May 1907. The serial numbers [inset detail] on the frame, backstrap and trigger guard match which together with the provenance of the letter make this a desirable collectors item and a piece of Browning history.

Above: An example of the Low Wall rifle with a vernier target sight.

WINCHESTER MODEL 1885 VARIANTS

Above: Model 1885 Express Rifle with a part round/part octagonal barrel chambered for the larger and heavier .50-111 Express ammunition.

Above: Model 1885 Express Rifle with round barrel and chambered for the British-made .50 Eley Express round.

Above: Express rifle chambered for the .40 Express round with a 30-inch casehardened round barrel and light walnut stock.

Above: A magnificent specimen with a 25 3/4 inch .32-40 caliber barrel, full Schutzen stock with Laudensack cheekpiece, and a Winchester palm-rest. The woodwork is high quality walnut, with discreet checkering on the forend and pistol grip.

WINCHESTER MODEL 1885 MUSKETS

As with all previous Winchester models there was a muzzleloading version of the Model 1885.

This one is a High Wall Second Model Musket in .45-70 caliber with a 32-inch round barrel, which was shipped from the Winchester factory in 1895.

A Low Wall version in .25-20 WCF caliber and 27-inch barrel; thought to be the only known musket in this caliber.

The vast majority of Model 1885 Low Wall muskets were in .22 short caliber as this one. Note the Lyman sight mounted on the receiver which was standard for these rifles.

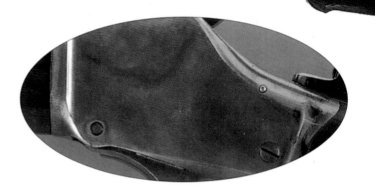

Above: Personal George C.Schoyen Winchester Model 1885 High wall Target Rifle with scope. Schoyen used this rifle to win the Denver Rifle Club Gold Championship Medal in 1895. Schoyen was a master barrel maker and gunsmith who built custom made rifles in his workshop in Denver, Colorado in the late 1800s. He favored single shot guns and specialized in Schutzen styles.

Winchester Model 1886 Lever-Action Repeater

Browning's next two designs were repeaters with tubular magazines, but although both were patented (U.S. Patents 261,667/1882 and 282,839/1883) neither went into production. The next, however, more than made up for this and was the Winchester Model 1886 (U.S. Patent 306,577/1884) which was manufactured from 1886 to 1935 and then in slightly modified form as the Model 71 from 1936 to 1957; a total production of 203,261 over a period of 71 years. The action featured a lever-activated sliding vertical lock and a tubular magazine, with an exposed hammer and mechanical safety. It was produced in many forms, calibers and weights during its long production run.

Left: Photographic portrait of Geo C. Schoyen from the Post studio in Denver.

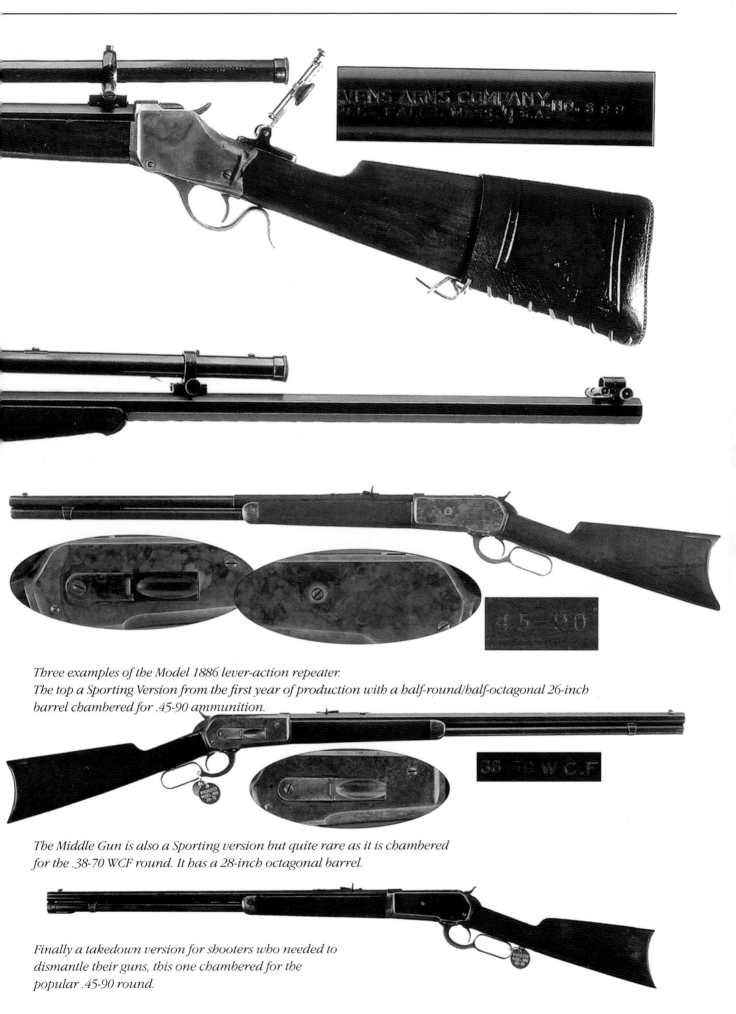

Three examples of the Model 1886 lever-action repeater.
The top a Sporting Version from the first year of production with a half-round/half-octagonal 26-inch barrel chambered for .45-90 ammunition.

The Middle Gun is also a Sporting version but quite rare as it is chambered for the .38-70 WCF round. It has a 28-inch octagonal barrel.

Finally a takedown version for shooters who needed to dismantle their guns, this one chambered for the popular .45-90 round.

VARIANTS OF THE WINCHESTER MODEL 1886

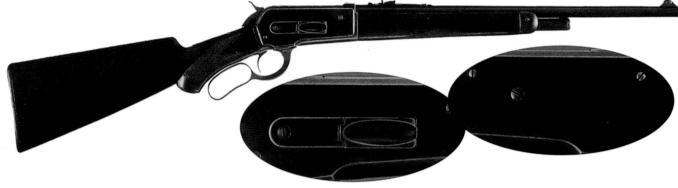

Model 1886 Lightweight with a half-length magazine and cut-back forend and a shortened 20-inch barrel.

An extra Lightweight in .45-70 caliber, with a 22-inch round barrel, half magazine and shotgun-style butt plate.

In keeping with Winchester tradition this is the musket version of the 1886, one of only 350 ever made. It has a 30-inch barrel and is chambered for .45-70 and complete with original bayonet.

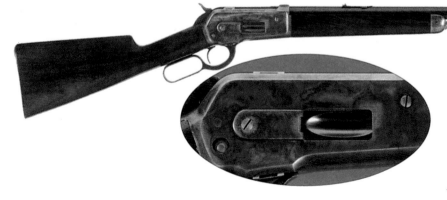

A model 1886 chambered for the .50 Express round. It has a 26-inch round barrel with a half magazine, shotgun butt and a straight grip. A special order exported to London in 1892 and bearing London proof marks it is thought that this gun was intended for hunting in some far-flung part of the British Empire.

Above: The Model 1886 was slightly modified and remarketed as the Browning Model 71 from 1936 to 1957.

Winchester Model 1890 Pump-Action Repeater

John Browning was granted U.S. Patent 385,238/1888 on this exceptional weapon in the ever-popular .22 caliber; it was his first pump-action repeater design and also the first such to be produced by Winchester. A vast improvement on previous designs, it had a positive feed mechanism and a tubular magazine which housed between eleven and fifteen rounds depending on type.

There were three families of this repeater, starting with the original Model 1890 which was in production from 1890 to 1932. It was made in four calibers which were not interchangeable: .22 Long, .22 Long Rifle, .22 Short and .22 Winchester Rimfire (WRF), the latter being designed specifically for use in this weapon. The Model 1890 was popular with small-game hunters and serious target shooters, but, with a selling price of $16, was also extensively used in shooting galleries, such that for much of the general public the name Winchester meant Browning's Model 1890 and was synonymous with fairground shooting.

Some 849,000 Model 1890s were produced, followed,

Winchester Model 1890 A First Model made in 1891 with a solid frame and chambered for .22 short rounds.

This Second Model with the takedown frame is a case-hardened version also with .22 chambering.

Later Second Model with a blued frame chambered for .22 WRF ammunition.

Above: Annie Oakley poses with her Winchester Model 1892 rifle which was essentially an updated Model 1873 using a scaled down version of Browning's Model 1886 action.

between 1906 and 1932, by the Model 06, which accepted all .22 rounds except .22 WRF; 848,000 were made. This was succeeded in production in 1932 by the Model 62, which continued the line with only minor changes to the barrels and sights; production ended in 1958 after 409,475 had been manufactured. Thus, the total life span of this design was 69 years, with well over two million produced.

Winchester Model 1892 Lever-Action Repeater

The Model 1892 was developed from the Model 86, and was, in essence a simpler and lighter version, intended for smaller caliber cartridges, ranging from .44 at the top end down to .25. It was produced in three basic versions – Models 1892, 53 and 65 – and remained in production until 1941 by which time just over one million had been manufactured. It was widely used around the world, being found in such disparate places as the North Pole with Admiral Perry and in the jungles of Brazil where it proved to be particularly popular with rubber planters.

Winchester Model 1894 Lever-Action Repeater

Probably the most famous and beloved sporting rifle in history, the Winchester Model 1894 (U.S. Patent 524,702/1894) was originally designed by John M. Browning to fire black powder rounds, but was quickly

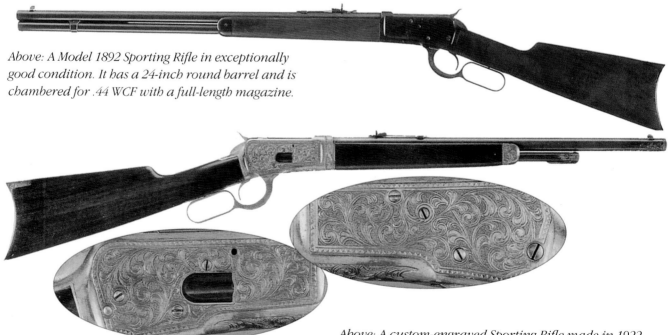

Above: A Model 1892 Sporting Rifle in exceptionally good condition. It has a 24-inch round barrel and is chambered for .44 WCF with a full-length magazine.

Above: A custom-engraved Sporting Rifle made in 1922. It has had 4 inches cut off the barrel making it into a carbine. The engraving is unusually deep cut and covers the frame, receiver and forend cap.

A good example of the Model 1892 Saddle-Ring Carbine with a 20-inch round barrel.

The Trapper's Carbine only had a 14-inch barrel.

An early production Model 1894 Sporting Rifle with a 26 inch barrel chambered for Winchester's smokeless .30-30 cartridge.

Takedown Version of the Model 1894.

Model 1894 engraved in the 1970s by Angelo Bee with a vignette of two dogs and a bear on the left side and a moose on the right all inlaid with gold.

Model 1894 carbine chambered for .30-30 supplied to Canada for coastal protection during World War II.

adapted – principally by changing the barrels from mild steel to nickel steel – to handle the new smokeless cartridges. One such round was the .30-30, which led to one of the gun's most popular names, the Winchester Thirty-Thirty. The Model 1894 was produced in five main versions: Standard Sporting (26-inch barrel), Fancy Sporting (26-inch barrel), Extra-lightweight (22- or 26-inch barrel), Carbine (20-inch barrel) and Trapper (14-, 15-, 16- or 18-inch barrel). The tubular magazine held a maximum of eight rounds in the standard version and six in the Carbine version. The original Model 1894 remained in production until the 1990s and standard models were supplemented by numerous commemorative issues, with well over 2,500,000 being produced in total. Direct developments were the Model 55, a simplified version of the Model 1894, which was in production from 1924 to 1932, and the

Model 64, a further refinement of the Model 55, of which 67,000 were made between 1933 and 1957, followed by a further small number in 1972–3.

Winchester Model 1895 Lever-Action Repeater

The Model 1895 (U.S. Patent 549,345/1895) received a very public endorsement from Theodore Roosevelt, who declared it to be his favorite hunting rifle – no marketing manager in any era could ask for more! This rifle was designed by John M. Browning to meet demands for a sporting rifle which would fire the new smokeless hunting cartridges with their jacketed and sharp-nosed bullets, particularly the service rounds such as the .30-40 Krag, .37-72 Winchester, the British military .303 and others. It had

WINCHESTER MODEL 1895 LEVER-ACTION REPEATERS

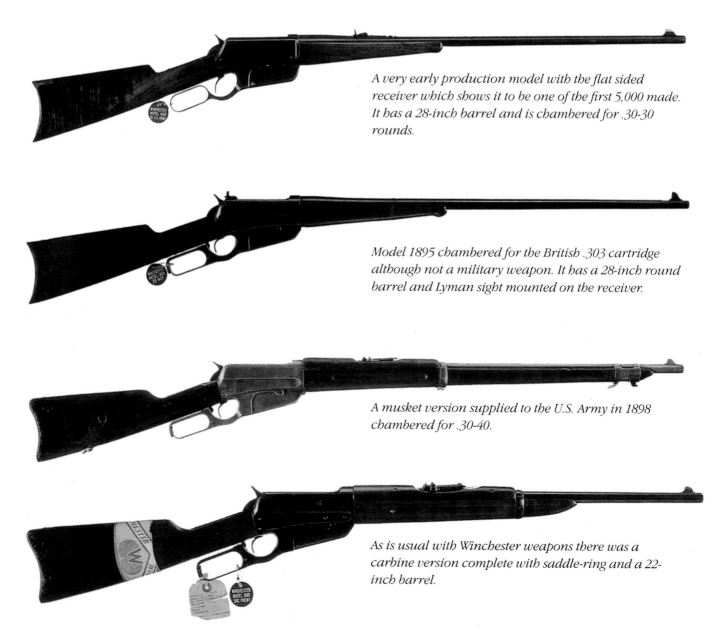

A very early production model with the flat sided receiver which shows it to be one of the first 5,000 made. It has a 28-inch barrel and is chambered for .30-30 rounds.

Model 1895 chambered for the British .303 cartridge although not a military weapon. It has a 28-inch round barrel and Lyman sight mounted on the receiver.

A musket version supplied to the U.S. Army in 1898 chambered for .30-40.

As is usual with Winchester weapons there was a carbine version complete with saddle-ring and a 22-inch barrel.

Above Theodore Roosevelt rests his trusty Model 1895 on the back of his kill –an African Rhino. The fact that it could stop such a beast spoke volumes for the gun's power.

a lever action and sliding vertical lock, but, unlike any other Winchester of its time, it had a fixed box magazine, which was intended to avoid the accidental explosions which sometimes occurred with pointed ammunition in a tubular magazine. There were four major versions – Sporting, Fancy Sporting, Carbine and Military Musket – with a variety of calibers, barrel lengths and weights.

The Military Musket, designated Model 1895S, was ordered during the Spanish-American War to rearm the United States' volunteer forces and state militias, which were then armed with very old-fashioned Springfield rifles using black-powder ammunition. The company sold 10,000 against this order, chambered for the then standard U.S. Army round, the .30-40 Krag. Some years later, in

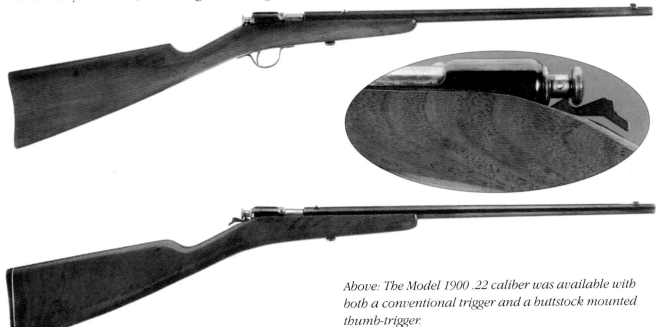

Above: The Model 1900 .22 caliber was available with both a conventional trigger and a buttstock mounted thumb-trigger.

1915–16, a further quantity was supplied to the Imperial Russian Army (see below). The Model 1895 was eventually phased out of production in 1931, by which time some 426,000 had been sold.

Winchester Model 1900 Single Shot .22 caliber

Some of John Browning's designs were among the most sophisticated automatic weapons of his day, but he was equally capable of turning his mind to products of the utmost simplicity, such as the Model 1900 Single Shot rifle, which fired either .22 Long Rifle or .22 Short Rifle rounds. This consisted of an 18-inch round barrel, bolt action, trigger group, and a single-piece gumwood stock. The simplicity resulted in a very low priced weapon, which was intended for use in short range gallery shooting (plinking) at informal targets such as blocks of wood or cardboard cut-outs, usually suspended from a cross-bar.

The Model 1900 was produced only for two years and was followed by the slightly improved Model 1902 and then the Model 1904 with a longer barrel and a lip on the fore-end of the stock. A rather different version was the

Above: Remington Model 8 Autoloading Rifle with Scope.

Right: Celebrated huntress Mrs. Briggs demonstrates the effectiveness of her Remington Model 8 in 1915 even without a scope!

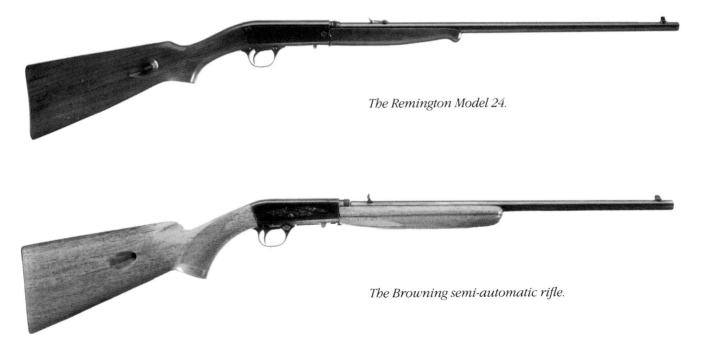

Above: The Remington Model 81 was a development of the Model 8.

Model 99 which was fired by depressing a button on the top of the buttstock with the thumb, thus dispensing with the normal trigger and guard. Despite costing a mere $3.50 it was not as popular in the United States as the other versions, with some 76,000 produced between 1904 and 1923, compared with 105,000 Model 1900, 640,000 Model 1902 and 303,000 Model 1904. For some unexplained reason, however, the Thumb-Trigger version proved to be particularly popular in Australia, where the bulk of Winchester's production was sold.

Remington Model 8 Semi-Automatic Rifle

This was John M. Browning's first self-loading (semi-automatic) rifle design and was granted U.S. Patent 659,786/1900. The Browning brothers then licensed United States' production to the Remington Arms Company, who produced it from 1906 to 1936 as the Model 8, and later to Fabrique Nationale in Belgium, who manufactured it from 1910 to 1931 as the Caliber .35 Automatic Rifle.

The barrel, which was surrounded by the recoil spring and an outer jacket, recoiled while locked to the bolt. The bolt was then unlocked and continued to the rear, extracting and ejecting the spent case as it went, for and then traveling forward to chamber the next round ready for the firer to pull the trigger. A hold-open device stopped the breechblock in the open position on detecting an empty magazine. The original production version had a fixed five-round magazine which was fed from the top using a clip, but later versions had a removable box magazine.

The Remington Model 8 continued in production until 1936, by which time some 60,000 had been built, and was then replaced by the Model 81, which was also known as the Woodmaster. This had minor improvements, increasing the weight from 7.75 pounds to 8 pounds, and remained in production until 1950. FN produced just under 5,000 Caliber .35 Automatic Rifles between 1910 and 1931; they weighed a few ounces more than the Model 8 and had some other minor differences such as modified sights.

The Remington Model 24.

The Browning semi-automatic rifle.

Above: Engraved Browning Grade II .22 Automatic Rifle.

Above: John M. Browning with the rifle that became both the Remington Model 24 and the Browning .22 Automatic. The characteristic side loading port on the buttstock is clearly visible.

Above: The FN Browning .22 caliber Automatic Rifle balanced on one finger. Taken from a pre-1914 advertisement.

FN .22 caliber Self-Loading Rifle (Remington Model 24/Browning .22 Automatic)

John Browning designed a number of .22 caliber rifles, of which the most successful was this self-loading weapon, which received U.S. Patents 1,065,341/1913, 1,065,342/1913 and 1,083,384/1914. Production rights for Europe and most of the rest of the world were immediately taken up by FN, whose production started in 1914, but was then interrupted by World War I and later by World War II. U.S. rights were purchased by Remington who manufactured it as the Model 24 from 1922 to 1935 and followed it with the longer-barreled Model 241 Speedmaster from 1935 until it was phased out in 1949. The weapon was then reintroduced on the U.S. market by the Browning Arms Company, although actual manufacture was at FN from 1956 to 1974 and at Miroku, Japan from 1976 onwards.

The .22 semi-automatic was a blowback-operated self-loader, with a take-down round barrel. In the original FN and Remington Model 24 versions the barrel was 19 inches long and the gun weighed 4.75 pounds, while the Remington 241 had a 23.5-inch barrel and weighed 6 pounds. All had a tubular magazine located in the buttstock; in the original FN version this was loaded through a port on the top of the stock, while the Remington 24 and all later versions had a side-loading port on the right side of the stock. The original Remington 24 fired only .22 Short Rifle, but was later modified to take .22 Long Rifle, as well, while all other versions can handle both rounds.

Winchester Model 1915/obr.1915g

When the Imperial Russian Army began to mobilize in August 1914 it was quickly realized that there were nothing like sufficient rifles to arm the millions of reservists. They quickly placed an order for Mosin-Nagant rifles with Winchester, but also ordered 300,000 of a modified Model 1895, which was chambered for the Russian 7.62 x 54 mm round, with appropriate sights and fitted for a 10-inch (later 16-inch) bayonet. It also had sling swivels and a charger guide. Known to Winchester as the Musket Model 1895, the Imperial Russian Army designated it the *Vintovka Vinchestya obr. 1915g* and when deliveries ended as a result of the 1917 Russian Revolution, between 293,000 and 299,000 had been accepted.

Above: A 28-inch barreled version of the Model 1895 in 7.63 mm which was shipped to the Russian Army in 1915. It has its original bayonet.

This one has a Grade II finish, with deluxe wood, high quality blue barrel and action, and light engraving on the side of the receiver.

Grade III finish comes with heavier engraving and checkered hand and pistol grips. This rifle was, in fact, one of a special edition of just sixty, made for the Browning Collectors Association.

The first is the basic model with blued barrel and receiver, and walnut stock-plain but perfectly serviceable.

FN .22 caliber Pump-Action Repeater

John Browning produced the prototype of this rifle in 1919, obtained U.S. Patent 1,424,553/1922 and then sold the licence to FN, with whom it entered production in 1922. It was a pump-action weapon with a 24-inch barrel in a take-down design and a tubular magazine holding fifteen .22 Short Rifle or eleven .22 Long Rifle rounds. Some 150,000 were produced in Belgium from 1922 to 1974, with a break for World War II, but, somewhat surprisingly, none of these reached the United States until the 1960s, when the Browning Arms Company imported some 3,000. The gun quickly earned the name The Trombone Rifle due to its slide action.

Designs never manufactured

As with all inventors, John M. Browning produced many prototypes that never got beyond the workshop doors, but he also produced a number of rifles whose production rights Winchester saw fit to buy, but then decided, for one reason or another, not to manufacture. The table shows 21 of those designs and they serve to illustrate some of the ideas he experimented with and the sheer breadth of his vision.

Most of these were lever-action weapons with different types of locking devices in John M. Browning's never-ending search for mechanical reliability combined with the other two essentials – smooth operation and safety. He also sought to make as many parts as possible serve more than one purpose, for example in Weapon A the lever also served as the locking lug, all of which, again, required prototypes and trials. He experimented not only with actions, but also with magazines (tubular, fixed box and detachable box) as well as with methods of loading and extraction.

Weapons H, K and L were particularly unusual in that they worked on the "pull apart" principle in which the weapon was constructed in two halves, the barrel and receiver forming one, and the breechblock, trigger group and buttstock the other, being linked by a tube. Having fired, the firer pulled the two halves apart, the distance, which was sufficient to extract the used case, being limited by a stop on the tube. The two halves were then pushed back together, picking up and chambering a new round as they did so and cocking the mechanism ready for firing. Although it now seems somewhat quaint, this must have appeared to be a worthwhile project at the time, and one which could only be proved or disproved by making and testing prototypes.

Weapon O in the table actually covers three prototypes, with very minor differences from each other. These formed part of John Browning's desire to perfect a really simple single-shot .22 caliber weapon for use by youngsters and for plinking.

Post-Browning Rifles

Following John M. Browning's untimely death at Herstal in 1926, development and production of the rifles he had designed continued, as it still does to the present day. In addition, new designs appeared which were marketed under the Browning Arms Company brand, although they were not actually manufactured in the United States.

SERIAL (see note)	CALIBER	ACTION	TYPE	US PATENT NUMBER	MAGAZINE YEAR	BARREL LENGTH	WEIGHT inches	pounds
A.	.38	Lever	Repeater	312,183	1885	Tubular	28	9.25
B.	.30	Lever	Repeater	324,296	1885	Tubular	28	9.25
C.	.45	Lever	Repeater	324,297	1885	Tubular	28	9.25
D.	.44	Pump	Repeater	367,336	1887	Tubular	20	5.87
E.	.45	Lever	Repeater	376,576	1888	Tubular	22	7.25
F.	.47-70	Lever	Repeater	428,887	1890	Box	28	8.12
G.	.44	Lever	Repeater	428,887	1890	Revolving	24	6.37
H.	.22	Pull-apart	Repeater	465,340		Tubular	21	5.5
I.	.45	Lever	Repeater	465,339	1891	Detachable box	28	9.12
J.	.30	Lever	Repeater	486,272	1892	Fixed box	32	9.12
K.	.30	Pull-apart	Repeater	486,273	1892	Fixed box	22.25	8.12
L.	.30	Pull-apart	Repeater	486,273	1892	Fixed box	32.75	9
M.	.30	Lever	Repeater	492,459	1893	Fixed box	22	8.12
N.	.30	Swing guard	Repeater	499,007	1893	Fixed box	30.75	8.62
O.	.22	Manual	Single-shot	511,677	1893	None	18.25	3.25
P.	.44	Lever	Repeater	499,005	1894	Tubular	23.25	6.87
Q.	.30	Pump	Repeater	545,672	1895	Fixed box	20	8.65
R.	.40	Lever	Repeater	545,671	1895	Tubular	25.5	7.37
S.	.236	Lever	Repeater	599,595	1898	Fixed box	28	7.62
T.	.30	Lever	Repeater	619,132	1899	Fixed box	28	7.62
U.	.30	Lever	Repeater	619,132	1899	Fixed box	28	7.75

Note: These serials are used only for identification in this book; they are neither Browning nor Winchester designations.

Browning Automatic Rifles (BAR)

THE BAR CURRENTLY IN PRODUCTION in the early 21st century is not related to John M. Browning's original design, but was the work of his son, Val, and entered production in 1967. Early manufacture took place entirely at Herstal in Belgium, but from 1977 onwards, while the components have still been produced by FN, final assembly has taken place in Portugal. In both cases, however, the end product was marketed in the United States under the Browning label.

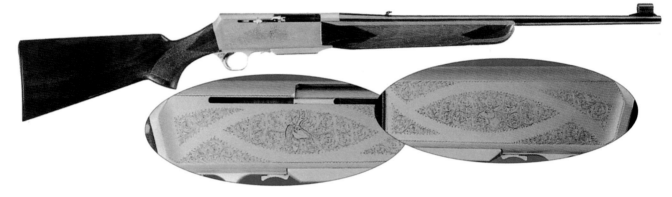

Grade III example in .243 caliber with antelope and deer engraving.

Grade IV example with elaborate big game scenes showing antelope and whitetail deer.

The Grade V has the animals inlaid with gold.

The BAR LongTrac with satin walnut stock.

The LongTrac Stalker with blued alloy receiver.

The Safari which has a one-piece ordnance steel receiver.

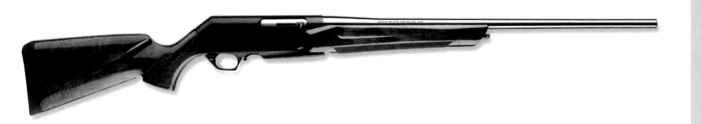

The ShortTrac.

Above: An example of the High Power Bolt-Action Rifle with Olympian finish in .22 caliber fitted with a Leupold Vari XIIc 4x12 scope.

This example has basic Safari finish and is made by Sako of Finland under license. It is chambered for .300 Winchester ammunition and has a 3x-9x Bushnell scope.

This example is made by FN and is chambered for .30-06, with a 22-inch barrel and a Leupold scope.

High-Power Bolt-Action Rifle

The High-Power Bolt-Action Rifle was a superior sporting rifle in a range of calibers from .458 Winchester Magnum down to .223 Remington, and in three grades, ranging from the standard, known as Safari, through Medallion to the highest, Olympian. Production started at Fabrique Nationale in 1959 employing Mauser actions, which were replaced in 1967 by FN Supreme actions in all calibers except .30-06 and .270, which retained the Mauser system. A second line was started by Sako of Finland in 1961, using a Sako-designed action. Both lines ceased production in 1975.

Browning Automatic Rifle (BAR)

The BAR is a gas-operated self-loading weapon, with a five-round box magazine, which can be recharged in place or removed. The rifle has been produced in a variety of chamberings, ranging from .243 up to .348 Magnum, and has been steadily developed over the years.

The original series was redesignated in the early 1970s into five numbered grades, the standard version becoming Grade I. The previous de luxe version became Grade II, and three new versions were introduced – Grades III through V – with ever more elaborate engraving and carving; there were also slight differences within each grade to denote standard or Magnum chambering. Grades II, III and V did not prove popular and were dropped after only three years. Another reorganization in the mid-1980s resulted in the Grade IV also being discontinued, while the standard version became the *Modèle Affût* and a new variant with special sights became the *Modèle Battue*. There have also been various special

editions including the North American Deer Rifle issue, which was chambered for .30-06 only.

Today, there are four models – ShortTrac, LongTrac, Lightweight Stalker and Safari – the latter also having an optional BOSS (Ballistic Optimizing Shooting System). The ShortTrac, LongTrac and Stalker versions have high-strength, aircraft-grade aluminum alloy receivers, while the heavier Safari has a one-piece ordnance-grade steel receiver. All have a composite trigger guard and magazine floorplate. The barrels, which are manufactured by FN in Belgium, are hammer-forged with a seven-lug rotary bolt system which engages tightly into the barrel to achieve maximum strength and accuracy, and both models have six shims to enable the firer to adjust the length of the stock. The ShortTrac is sold in five calibers – .270 WSM, 7 mm WSM, .300 WSM, .243 Winchester and .308 Winchester – while the LongTrac is sold in four calibers – .270 Win., .30-06 Springfield, 7 mm Remington Magnum and .300 Winchester Magnum. The ShortTrac, LongTrac and Safari are tapped for telescopic sights, but the Lightweight Stalker is fitted with open (iron) sights, the foresight consisting of a gold-headed blade dovetailed into a hooded ramp, while the backsight is ramp-mounted and click adjustable.

Model BBR

The Browning Model BBR entered manufacture at Miroku, Japan in 1978. It had a turning action, three-lug bolt, with a 24-inch barrel and a detachable box magazine, which was held in place by a hinged floorplate. The BBR was chambered for the .25-06, .270 Winchester, 7 mm Remington Magnum, .30-06 or .300 Winchester Magnum rounds and was eventually superseded by the A-Bolt in 1984.

Browning Model BBR with scope mounts and a sling strap.

Browning A-Bolt Rifles

THE BROWNING A-BOLT was developed by Miroku as an improved version of the Model BBR. Introduced in 1986, it is still in production in 2006 in a wide variety of chamberings, the free-floating barrel coming in three lengths (22, 24 or 26 inches) and there is a number of finishes. It has the same three-lug bolt action as the BBR in either long or short actions and is sold without sights, leaving the purchaser free to make his own arrangements; the magazine arrangement is the same as on the BBR and left-handed versions are available. The standard version is the Hunter and others currently available are the Mountain, Stalker, and Medallion, but there have been many variations and special issues over the years, two examples among many being the Big-Horn Sheep issue of 1986–7 made in .270 caliber only and with production limited to precisely 600, and the Pronghorn issue of 1987 in .243 caliber, with 500 made.

Above: The A-Bolt Medallion left handed version.

Above: A-Bolt Mountain with Mossy Oak finish.

Above: A-Bolt Stalker.

Above: A-Bolt Eclipse.

Above: A-Bolt Hunter.

Above: High Grade A-Bolt with Leupold Vari X II 3-9c scope.

Above: A-Bolt with Swarovski 3x-9x Habicht scope and composite stock.

Above: Boxed A-Bolt in .22 caliber.

Gold Medallion A-Bolt made by B.C.Miroku of Kochi, Japan.

Three examples of boxed A-Bolt rifles.

T-Bolt

The T-Bolt Model T-1 was produced by FN in Belgium, between 1965 and 1974. Chambered only for .22, it had a five-round magazine and a 22-inch barrel, and with an unusual straight-pull bolt, which gave the model its name. The T-Bolt T-2 was a higher-grade model with a checkered walnut stock and 24-inch barrel.

Browning T-Bolt left hand model in .22 caliber with Bushnell 4X scope.

A boxed example of the Model BLR.

The Model 81 BLR with a 20-inch barrel and 4 round detachable box magazine.

A similar model but with a 20-inch barrel chambered for .358 Winchester.

Model BLR/BLR-81

The BLR (Browning Lever-action Rifle) was designed by John M. Browning's son, Val, at the FN works in Herstal, and entered production at Miroku, Kochi, Japan in 1973, chambered for the .243 and .308 Winchester rounds. The trigger group is integral with the operating lever, which moves the bolt to the rear using a rack-and-pinion system. In 1982 the original BLR was replaced by the BLR-81 which had an improved action, and a lengthened straight butt wrist, but recent models have a curved pistol grip and a Schnabel-type forearm.

Buck Mark Rifles

THE BASIC CONCEPT OF THE BROWNING BUCK MARK rifle echoes some designs of the late 19th and early 20th centuries when a number of the heavier automatic pistols, such as the German Luger, could be fitted with clip-on stocks, transforming them into shoulder-fired weapons. This enabled them to be used at longer ranges and with greater accuracy than if fired by hand. In the case of the ultra-modern Buck Mark rifle, the design is based on the successful Browning Buck Mark semi-automatic .22 caliber pistol, but with a longer, heavier barrel, forearm grip, and the stock permanently attached by a unique open frame.

FEATURES OF BUCK MARK RIFLE

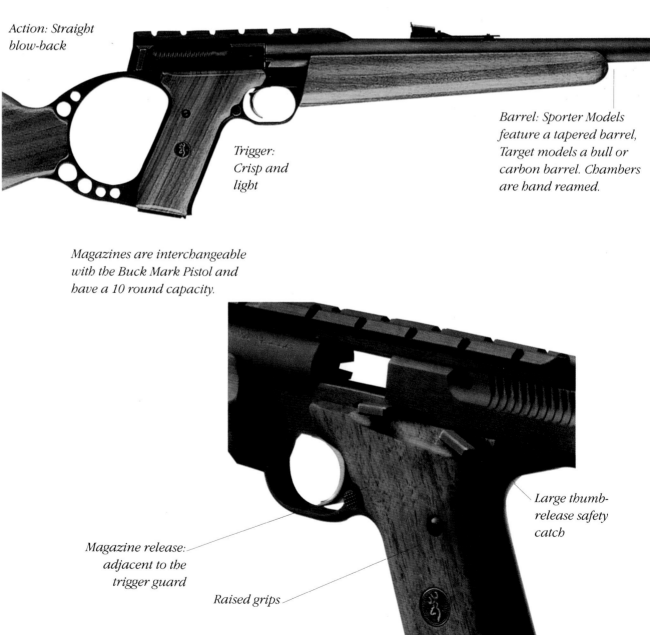

Frame: Machined out of a solid billet of aluminum

Sights Sporter Models feature a Truglo/Marbles fiber optic system

Action: Straight blow-back

Trigger: Crisp and light

Barrel: Sporter Models feature a tapered barrel, Target models a bull or carbon barrel. Chambers are hand reamed.

Magazines are interchangeable with the Buck Mark Pistol and have a 10 round capacity.

Large thumb-release safety catch

Magazine release: adjacent to the trigger guard

Raised grips

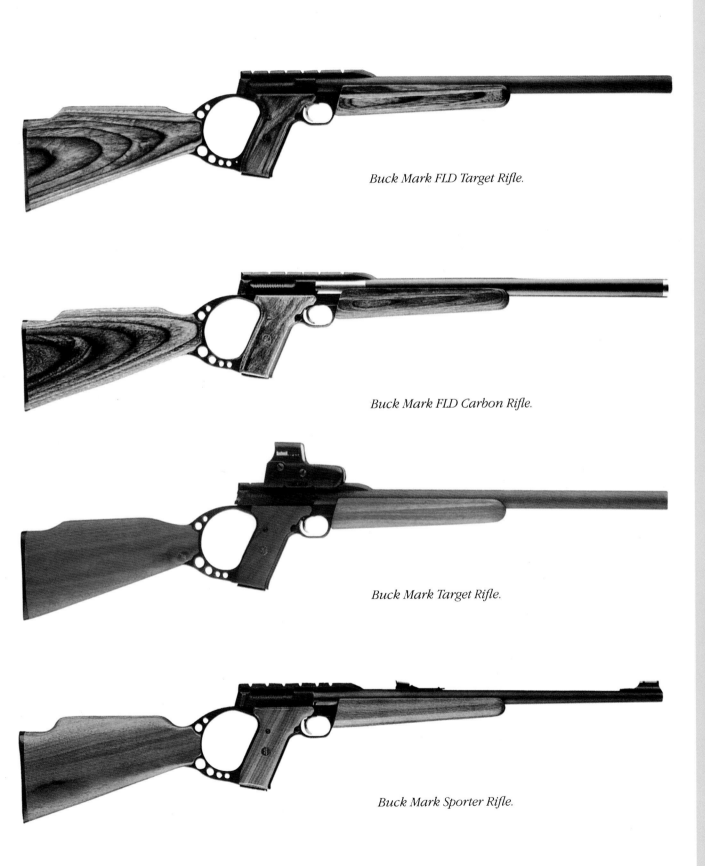

Buck Mark FLD Target Rifle.

Buck Mark FLD Carbon Rifle.

Buck Mark Target Rifle.

Buck Mark Sporter Rifle.

Buck Mark rifle

All models in the range have an 18-inch barrel, integral rail for mounting a telescopic sight and an eleven-round magazine in the pistol grip. There are three basic models. The Sporter is the standard, weighing 4 pounds 6 ounces, and fitted with a fiberoptic rear sight and muzzle-mounted foresight. The Target model has a bull-type barrel and weighing 5 pounds 6 ounces while the Carbon has a carbon composite barrel and weighs a mere 3 pounds 10 ounces. FLD versions of the Target and Carbon have gray laminated stock, pistol grips and forearm while others have conventional wooden furniture; all have aluminum frames.

Post-War .22 Caliber Rifles

A large number of .22 caliber rifles have appeared bearing the Browning label. Among the first were the 3,000 imported from Fabrique Nationale in the 1960s (see earlier) and these were followed between 1977 and 1982 by the BPR-22 (Browning Pump-action Rifle) with a 20.25-inch barrel and chambered for the .22 Magnum cartridge.

Semi-Automatic 22

Miroku still produces the original Browning self-loading design as the Browning Semi-Automatic 22 (SA-22). This is a blowback-operated rifle which can be taken down into two sections with a maximum length of 19 inches, making it ideal for packing and travelling. The 19-inch barrel is fitted with two iron sights and a beaver-tail forearm, while the buttstock contains a tubular magazine, loaded through a side port and with a capacity of twelve .22 Long Rifle rounds. There are two grades; Grade I is the standard, with American walnut furniture,

Above: Model BL-22 Grade II rifle.

Above: Boxed BL-22 with checkered stock and forend.

lightly engraved receiver and polished, blued finish to the receiver and barrel, while the Grade VI has more elaborately checkered and higher grade woodwork and a receiver with gold-plated engraved game scenes.

BL-22 and BL-17

Browning has also introduced a new series of lever-action rifles, the BL-22 and BL-17, with three grades in each of two calibers. The BL-22 models are chambered for all the traditional .22 cartridges, with the exception of .22 Magnum, but the BL-17 fires the totally new Hornady .17 Mach 2 (.17M2) round, which consists of a slightly lengthened .22LR rimfire case necked down to hold a .17 caliber Hornady bullet. Using a 24-inch barrel, the muzzle velocity of this new bullet is 2,100 ft/sec (1,522 mph or Mach 2), which is some 70 percent faster than a .22LR, so that the new round's trajectory is essentially flat, with a considerably reduced time of flight resulting in greater accuracy. The three grades in each caliber differ in finish, decoration and sighting, but all feature a short-throw lever-action with a 33-degree arc. All are also fitted with a tubular magazine which houses: BL-22 – fifteen .22 Long Rifle, seventeen .22 Long; or twenty-two standard .22 (or any combination of those rounds); BL-17 – fifteen rounds of .17M2 only.

Limited Editions

In addition to its extensive catalogue range, the Browning company has also marketed a large number of special editions in strictly limited production runs, which are intended to mark a memorable anniversary (usually 100th or 200th) or simply to enable enthusiasts to get their hands on a great design, but manufactured by modern methods.

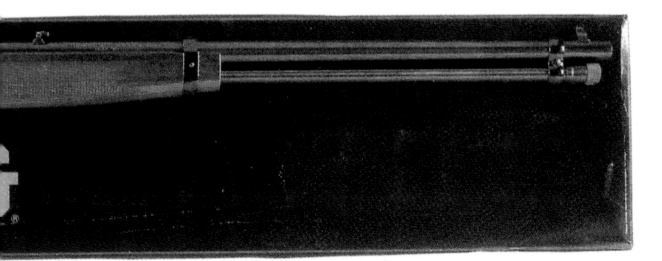

Above: The Model 53 kept the Winchester tradition alive.

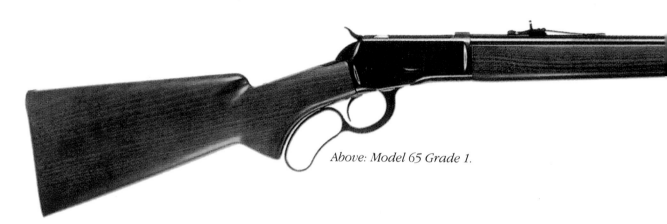

Above: Model 65 Grade 1.

Model 53

The Model 53 was produced in the early 1990s with a limited run of 5,000 only. It was a reproduction of the Winchester Model 53 of 1924, which was, itself, a marginal development of the Winchester Model 1892.

Model 65

The original Model 65 was a development of the Model 53, which was, in its turn, based on the legendary Model 1892, and was in production from 1933 to 1947. It was a fine gun but was produced in only small numbers: 5,704 over 14 years. It had a lever action and was chambered for

various rounds, but the special edition Model 65, produced in 1989 only, was chambered for just one round, the .218 Bee cartridge. Only 3,500 were made, plus another 1,500 of the Model 65 High Grade, which had top quality wooden furniture, gold-inlaid engravings of hunting scenes and a gold-plated trigger.

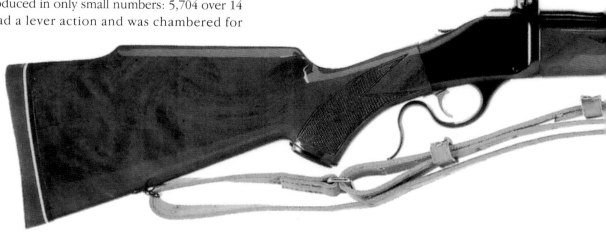

Model 71

The original Winchester Model 71 was a slightly modified version of the Model 1886, rechambered for the .348 Winchester cartridge, of which 43,267 were manufactured between 1936 and 1957. This was reintroduced as a special edition in 1986–7, still for the .348 cartridge, in two models, a rifle with a 24-inch barrel, and a carbine with a 20-inch barrel, each of them in two grades, Grade I and High Grade. Total production was 13,000.

Jonathan Browning Centennial Mountain Rifle

John M. Browning's designs were not the only ones to be honored and in 1978 the company marked the centenary of John's father's death with a special edition of 2,000 replicas of Jonathan Browning's Mountain Rifle design. Intended to meet the requirements of black powder enthusiasts, this rifle was produced in .45 or .54 caliber, with 1,000 of the standard design and 1,000 of the higher Centennial grade.

Model 1885

Miroku of Japan has produced several modern versions of the Model 1885. The first of these appeared in the 1970s under the designation Browning B-78 and was chambered for the .22-50, 6 mm Remington, .270 Winchester or .30-06 rounds. Miroku then produced one thousand in .45-70 caliber as a special edition to mark the U.S. bicentennial. A commercial model was then developed, which entered production in 1988 although it was actually designated the M1885. Other versions included High Wall, Low Wall, Low Wall Hunter (with tang sight), Black Powder, and High Wall Traditional Hunter.

Express Rifle

This unusual superposed (over/under) gun was produced in several versions, the first appearing in 1978. Designated the Continental Set, this comprised two sets of barrels, one pair of over/under rifle barrels, chambered for .30-06, the other a pair of shotguns barrels in 20-gauge. Some 500 were produced in a very limited run between 1978 and 1986. This was followed by the Express Rifle which had a pair of rifle barrels only, in either .270 Winchester or .30-06.

Model 1885 of 1988 went right back to the company's roots.

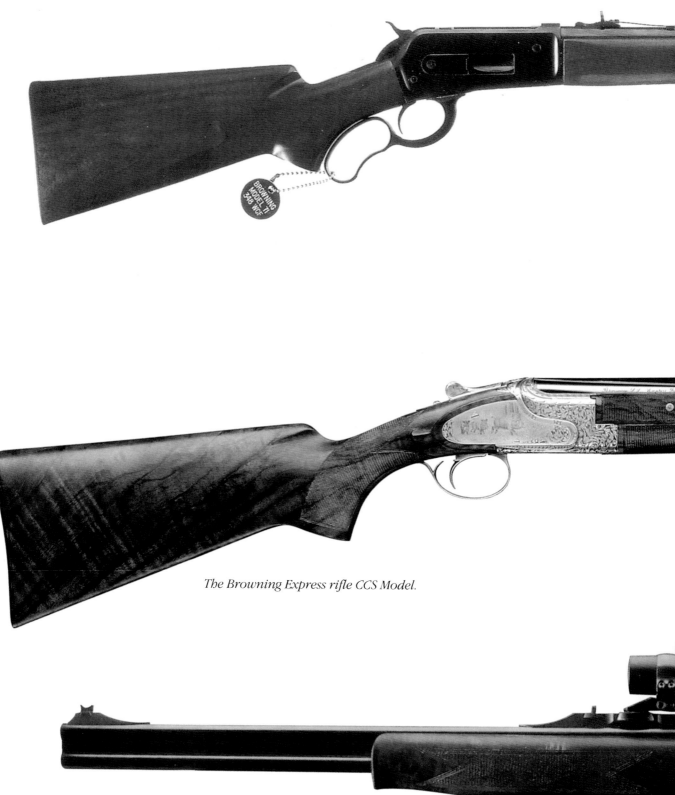

The Browning Express rifle CCS Model.

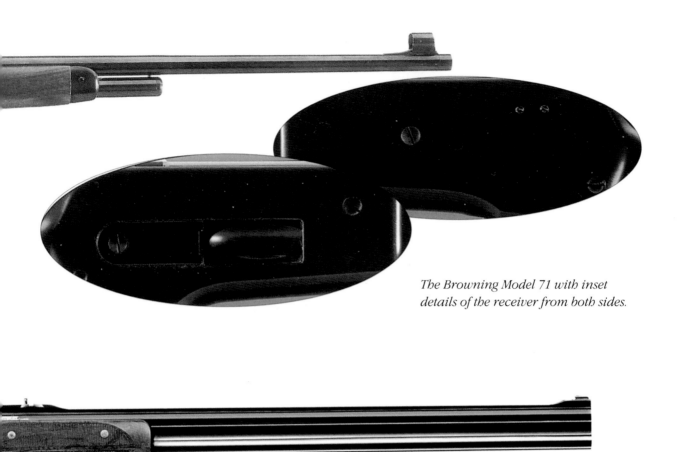

The Browning Model 71 with inset details of the receiver from both sides.

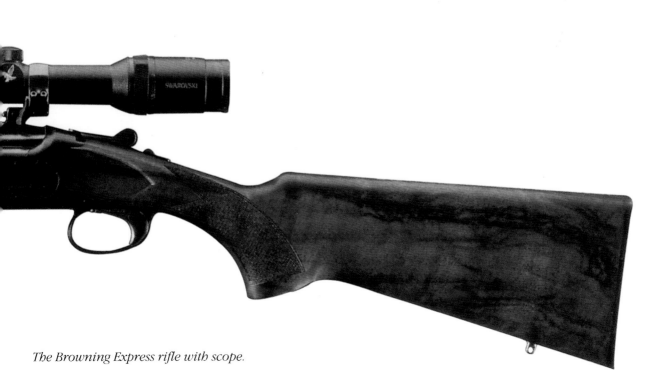

The Browning Express rifle with scope.

Chapter Four

Shotguns

THE CONTRIBUTION MADE by John Moses Browning to the development of the shotgun was greater than that made by any other single individual in history. One of the keys to this success was that he was an ardent shooter himself, which meant that not only was he able to look at matters from the user's point-of-view, but he was also able to test his latest ideas and prototypes in the hills and fields around Ogden, as well

Above: Model 1887 in 12 gauge with a 30-inch barrel made in 1891.

The Winchester 1887 shotgun was used by the Texas Rangers. They are seen here loading one.

Above: This 1892-built one has a 30-inch, 10 gauge barrel.

as in the many competitions he entered. Even with his interest in rifles, pistols and machine guns, he seems to have had a particular love for shotguns, not only for hunting but also for competitive shooting, so that it is not surprising that his mind should have turned to producing an ever-improving series of designs.

Winchester Models 1887 and 1901 Lever-Action Repeating Shotguns

Shortly after his Single-Shot Rifle had been accepted by Winchester in 1883, Browning turned his attention to shotguns. At the time (the mid-1880s) there were already a number of multi-shot shotguns on the market, but these all functioned by means of multiple barrels. Both single- and double-barreled shotguns were used mainly by sportsmen and hunters and by competitive shots, but they were also proving to be of increasing interest to both lawmen and criminals in the Old West, where their performance against human targets at short ranges or in confined spaces was devastating. All of these guns had to be "broken-open" to reload, and even though experts could do this very quickly, many were looking for a shotgun which would hold more than two rounds, as well as being quick and easy to reload.

Browning set about solving this problem and the outcome was his lever-action repeater, which, while not the first such to be marketed in the United States (there had been earlier, but very short-lived models by Colt, Spencer and Roper), it was nevertheless the first to

achieve popular acceptance and significant sales. U.S. patent 336,287/1886 was duly awarded and John sold the manufacturing rights to Winchester, who quickly readied it for production and had it on sale the following year as their Model 1887.

The Model 1887 was sold in either 10- or 12-gauge and held four shells in the tubular, under-barrel magazine, plus one in the chamber. The Model 1887 remained in production until 1899 when it was withdrawn and redesigned to take smokeless powder loads, returning to sale in 1902 (but only in 10-gauge) as the Winchester Model 1901, which remained in production until 1920. Total production of the Model 1887 was 64,855, while the Model 1901 reached 13,500.

It was inevitable that the new weapon should have attracted the attention of men who habitually carried shotguns in their work, particularly those in the Old West, who found the lever-action greatly superior to the double-barrel shotgun. A major advantage was the increase in the number of shells, which was officially five – four in the magazine and one in the carrier – but it was quickly found that an additional shell could be held in the chamber, bringing the total up to six. This, allied to sawing off the barrel to give easier stowage (and also, in some cases, shortening the butt, as well), produced a weapon that Westerners could use to great advantage. Having observed these developments, in 1898 Winchester produced a riot gun version of the Model 1887 with a 20-inch barrel, which, although intended for law enforcement agencies, was also on sale to the general public.

Above and Left: A special order Model 1893 with a Damascus barrel, deluxe flamegrain walnut stock with a checkered pistol grip. Only a few of these models survive.

Winchester Model 1893 Pump-Action Repeating Shotgun

John Browning's interest was never confined to one type of weapon nor to one method of operation, and with his lever-action shotgun successfully launched he turned to a new action, which led to a new design, patented under U.S. 441,390/1890. Again it was sold to Winchester, who put it on the market in 1894 as the Model 1893. Like the lever-action weapon, this had a tubular magazine under the barrel, but this time it was operated by a sliding forearm, usually referred to as pump action or slide action, but also sometimes called trombone action. It was made in 12-gauge only, with a five-round magazine (plus one in the chamber), top ejection and either 30-inch or 32-inch barrels. It was in production for only three years and was then replaced by the Model 1897.

Winchester Model 1897 Pump-Action Repeating Shotgun

The Model 1897 was a modified version of the Model 1893, which could be taken down for storage and transportation. It had a longer chamber, side ejection, improved stock and was built around a more robust frame than the Model 1893. It achieved great popularity in the United States and the standard version remained in production until 1957 – an astonishing 60 years.

There were at least eight versions. The Standard, Trap, Pigeon and Brush were all produced in either 12-gauge (30-inch barrel) or 16-gauge (28-inch barrel), with minor differences according to their intended function. The Brush Gun was also made in a takedown version. The Tournament was made in 12-gauge only with a 30-inch barrel. The Riot Gun was made in 12-gauge, with a 20-inch barrel, and fired buckshot. The Trench Gun was very similar to the Riot Gun but had a slotted barrel handguard and a bayonet lug. Production years were: Standard 1897–1957; Trap 1897–1931; Special Trap 1932–1939; Pigeon 1897–1939; Brush 1897–1931; Riot 1898–1935;

Above: A Model 1897 Trench Gun for use in close combat in World War I complete with bayonet.

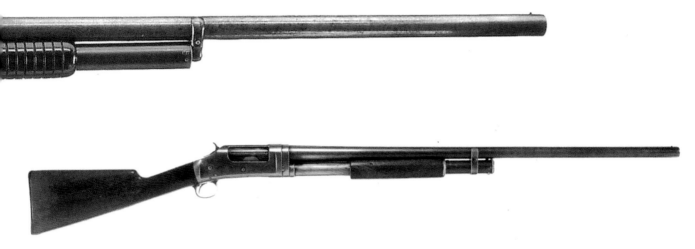

Above: Standard version of the 1897 Pump-Action shotgun with 30-inch barrel in 12 gauge.

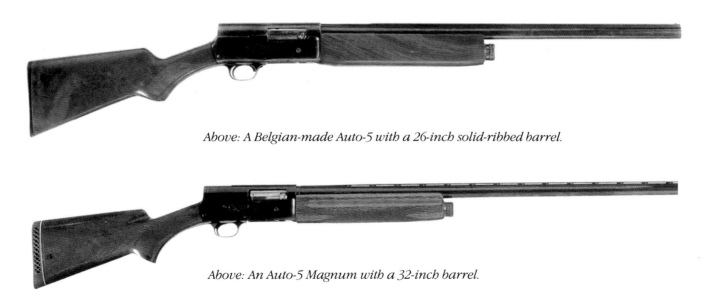

Above: The Model 1897 trench gun was reinstated in World War II.

Tournament 1910–1931; Standard Trap 1931–1939 and Trench 1920–1935.

Browning Automatic-5 (Auto-5)

One of the most famous shotgun designs of all time, the Browning Auto-5 was not only the very first reliable automatic shotgun, but was also so successful that it remained in full production in the same, basically unaltered, design for 96 years – spanning virtually the entire 20th century. Indeed, it is still available to special order. This is a truly remarkable record for any invention. Browning filed his first patent application for what he termed a "Recoil Operated Firearm" in May 1899, shortly after his return from two years missionary work for his church, and it seems virtually certain that,

Above: A Belgian-made Auto-5 with a 26-inch solid-ribbed barrel.

Above: An Auto-5 Magnum with a 32-inch barrel.

Auto-5 Sweet Sixteen 16 gauge shotgun with a 28-inch barrel.

The Gold Classic was a limited edition of 500 and had a bust of John M. Browning engraved on it.

despite his religious commitments, the basic ideas must have been turning over in his mind during that enforced sabbatical away from the drawing board and workshop. While this and later self-loading shotguns are referred to as 'automatic,' they are actually semi-automatic weapons which need a pull on the trigger to fire each shell.

Browning's new shotgun was covered by four U.S. patents: 659,507/1900 for the basic gun design, 689,283/1901 for the final design, 710,094/1902 covering a number of component improvements, and 812,326/1906 detailing further improvements to the mechanism. To design an automatic shotgun was revolutionary enough, but John Browning carried out this work at a time when smokeless powder was being introduced and manufacturers had not yet solved the problems of variations in load, which could lead to catastrophic events such as split barrels. Indeed, the first automatic shotgun to be sold in the United States was made by a French company named Clair of St Etienne; it was sold from 1895 onwards but was extrememely unreliable for this very reason. Such difficulties taxed manually-loaded shotgun designers, but they were even more of a problem in an automatic action, yet John M. Browning solved them all, primarily because of his recent experience in designing and developing automatic pistols and rifles.

Left: John M. Browning poses with one of his most recognizable creations – the Auto-5.

John Browning's autoloader used the long recoil system, where, on firing, the gasses from the cartridge caused the barrel and bolt, which at this stage were locked together, to recoil over a distance marginally greater than the length of the shell. At this point the bolt was held back while the barrel was released and driven forwards again by the return spring. The used shell case was retained momentarily by the bolt and as soon as the chamber had uncovered it, was ejected. The bolt was then released to travel forward, cocking the action and chambering a new shell as it went. The gun was then ready to be fired again.

This is, of course, an oversimplification of a complicated process. The shells were housed in a tubular magazine beneath the barrel, which housed five rounds – hence the name "Auto-5." The other name for this shotgun is "Old Humpback," derived from the unique and instantly recognizable shape of the the vertical back to the action.

As described in Chapter One, the design was originally offered to Winchester, then to Remington, and, finally, to Fabrique Nationale of Belgium. The latter could not contain their enthusiasm and had the new design in production by 1903, and under the terms of the initial contract, the first batches off the production line were shipped to the Browning brothers in Ogden, Utah, in September of that year. These early batches were in 12-gauge only and were in four grades of finish and four barrel lengths: 26, 28, 30 and 32 inches. The original models were: Standard (also known as Regular), Trap, Messenger and Two-Shot Automatic. The term "Messenger Gun" was in common usage at the time and denoted a

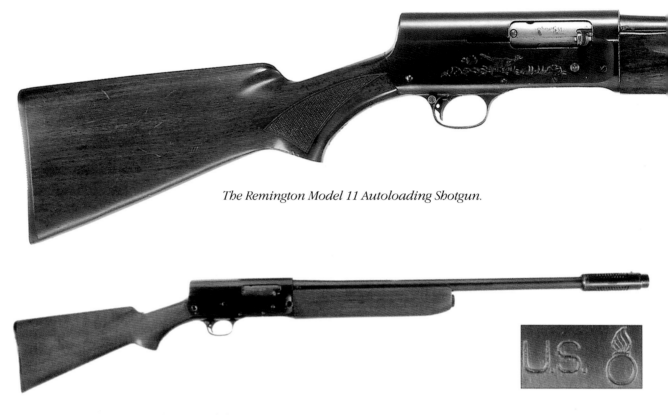

The Remington Model 11 Autoloading Shotgun.

Another U.S. Army variant with a 20-inch barrel for riot use.

Model 11 converted to train Army Air Corps gunners during World War II.

shotgun with a shortened barrel, which was intended for self-defense by people such as guards, couriers and messengers. The Two-Shot Automatic was produced to meet the needs of people such as the police who considered that the full complement of shells was unnecessary in law enforcement and a smaller number was preferable.

In late 1903 Browning renegotiated his contract with FN and was released from his obligation to import Auto-5s into the United States, while FN continued to hold the license to market the weapon in the whole world, less the United States. Browning then leased the U.S. license to Remington, who started production in 1905, changing its name to the Model 11 in 1911 and going on to manufacture some 300,000 of all types of the Browning design before production ended in 1948. The company also produced some 45,000 "American Browning Auto-5s" which were

made for the Browning Company and sold under the latter's label between 1940 and 1944, when supplies from Belgium ceased due to the German invasion.

Fabrique Nationale restarted production of the Auto-5 almost as soon as the factory was liberated in 1944, but on a very limited basis, with full-scale production not under way again until 1946–7. The Browning Company then ended the contract with Remington in 1947 and began to import direct from FN again. This Belgian production continued until 1976 in either 12- or 16-gauge, with a wide variety of barrel lengths, chokes and embellishments. Versions optimized for particular roles included Lightweight, Magnum, Skeet, Trap, Sweet Sixteen and Buck Special. FN also marked production of the two-millionth post-war Auto-5 with 2,500 of a very special commemorative issue, produced between 1971 and 1974. Production then moved to Miroku in Japan in 1976,

*Two backwoods hunters. One has bagged a jack rabbit
with his Remington Model 11.*

since when FN has continued to produce occasional batches of Auto-5s, such as the Classic with high-grade etching (5,000 produced), the even more select and expensive Gold Classic (500 produced), and a Centenary model in 1989. Miroku eventually phased this outstanding weapon out of production in 1999, the last batch of 1,000 weapons being the "Auto-5 Final Tribute Limited Edition."

Once U.S. troops had become involved in World War I they rapidly gained experience of trench warfare, which led to an operational requirement for a gun to be used in close-quarter combat when clearing enemy trenches. This needed to produce a high volume of fire at very short range, a task for which an autotmatic shotgun was ideal. But, apart from firing multiple shells, the U.S. Army also stated that the weapon needed a bayonet. Such use required one hand to be grasping the barrel, which by then could be very hot, and so demanded modification to the basic design. These requirements were met by Remington by adding a jacket around the barrel, which was both cool to the touch and also incorporated the bayonet lug.

The Messenger Gun category of the early 1900s was intended for close-combat situations, as opposed to all other civilian versions of the Auto-5 which were designed for sporting use. However, a number of criminals in the Twenties and Thirties found the sporting Auto-5 a very handy weapon and adapted it for their own nefarious purposes, usually by sawing off some of the barrel and shortening the butt, while some also added a forward handgrip, similar to that found on the Thompson sub-machine gun. Bonnie Parker, of "Bonnie and Clyde" fame, owned a number of 20-gauge Remington Model

11s with barrels shortened to between 14 and 17 inches and the butts sawn off behind the pistol grip.

Stevens Model 520 Pump-Action Shotgun

Despite all the work he was doing on automatic weapons in the early years of the 20th century, John Browning still found the time to develop another pump-action shotgun. He applied for a patent in 1903, which, although he had already sold the production rights, took some two years to process, being eventually granted as U.S. Patent 781,765//1905. The rights were bought by the Savage Arms and Tool Company of Chicopee Falls,

The Stevens Model 520-30 was based on yet another Browning patent.

The 520 developed into the Model 620.

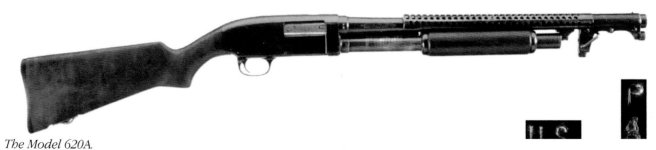

The Model 620A.

The Remington Model 17 Slide Action Shotgun.

Massachusetts who were very quick to place it in production, with early examples in the shops in early 1904 as the Stevens Model 520.

The Model 520 was a hammerless, takedown weapon, with a five-round tubular magazine under the barrel, around which was wrapped the hand-operated slide; there was also space for another round in the chamber. It was originally marketed in 12-gauge, but later also appeared in 16- and 20-gauge, with barrels varying in length from 20 to 32 inches; it weighed approximately 7 pounds 12 ounces. The Model 520 had a vertical rear end to the receiver and this was changed to a more streamlined appearance in the Model 620, which otherwise differed little from its predecessor. The Model 520 was manufactured from 1904 to 1932 and the Model 620 from 1927 to 1955.

The Model 520 was the basis of the Stevens Trench Gun, which, like the Auto-5, was developed to meet the requirements of the U.S. Army in France in 1917–18. This had a 20-inch barrel surrounded by a perforated metal handguard, which was fitted with a Stevens-designed adapter for the M1917 bayonet, or, with minimal modification, for the M1905 bayonet. This trench-gun arrived too late to be accepted and few were produced, only to be placed in storage. These were immediately bought by the U.S. Army on the otutbreak of World War II and some were still in service during the Vietnam War.

Remington Model 17 Pump-Action Shotgun

John Browning had a long history of pump-action designs, and this one, granted U.S. Patent 1,143,170/1915, was to be his last. Manufacturing rights were leased to Remington, but due to the war production did not actually start until 1921, when it was marketed as the Remington Model 17. It was a takedown design, but showing yet again innovation created by John's desire for constant improvement. In this design, it was only the barrel which was removed, being secured to the gun by interrupted threads, needing only a quarter-turn to attach/detach, and being locked securely in place by a stud. Simple to use, the locking system was also easier and cheaper for the manufacturer to produce.

The Model 17 was manufactured in 20-gauge only, with barrel lengths of 26, 28, 30 and 32 inches. The tubular magazine under the barrel held five shells, with a sixth in the chamber. Once sales of the sporting shotgun were

under way, Remington turned to a riot-gun version, the Model 17R, with a 20-inch barrel and a four-shell magazine. One unusual feature of this weapon was the rapid-fire option, where if the trigger was held back the gun would fire every time the forearm was pumped. The Model 17R did not sell well and was quickly succeeded by the Model 17 Special Police Gun (also known more succinctly as the Police Special) which was based on the sporting gun and designed to be fired from the hip, with one hand on the pistol grip and the other on the forearm; it could be fired equally well by right- or left-handed shooters. It was particularly valued by the police for close-quarter work in confined spaces, such as stairwells, and for the ease with which it could be concealed, since the 15-inch barrel and the pistol grip (which replaced the conventional butt) resulted in a length of no more than 25 inches and an unloaded weight of 4 pounds 8 ounces. Manufacture ended in 1933, although for some years afterwards some police departments in the United States converted normal Model 17s or 17Rs to Police Special configuration, with the shortened barrel and pistol grip. As with so much of John Browning's work, as soon as the patent expired other companies used the same basic design to produce "new" weapons bearing their own logo.

Fabrique Nationale Superposed Shotgun

In the early 20th century, a number of inventors had designed shotguns with two barrels one above the other (known as either superimposed or superposed). It was John Browning, however, who brought the concept to perfection in what would turn out to be his last major invention.

The Superposed shotgun was patented in the United States (1,578,638–9/1926), entered production at Fabrique Nationale in 1927 and reached the U.S. market in small numbers from 1931 onwards. It is loaded by breaking the weapon, inserting two shells and closing it again. Sighting is easy since, unlike a side-by-side shotgun, there is only one sighting plane. In John Browning's original design there were two triggers, one for each barrel, but his son, Val, later designed a single trigger. In the initial version, one barrel was fired on the first pull, the other on the second, while in the second version the barrel to be fired is selected by a thumb switch. These single trigger devices removed the need for the shooter to move his finger from one trigger to the other.

Original Superposed models were designated B25, B125 and the modern production versions B26, B27 and B127. Pre-war production was in 12-gauge only and four grades, One, Pigeon, Diana and Midas, and ceased in 1940 after some 17,000 had been produced. Post-war production restarted at Fabrique Nationale in 1947 with new chamberings added, so that the line-up now comprised 12-, 20- and 28-gauge, but with the quality now being denoted by Roman numerals from I through VI. Then in 1959–60 the grades reverted to the pre-war naming system, but with Pointed added between Pigeon and Diana, and .410 bore added to the chamberings. Since then production has continued down to today's Citori series, made by Miroku of Japan since 1973 in the usual wide selection of finishes.

Numerous limited editions have been offered, including: Exhibition grades from 1973–77, Superlight in 1967–80, Bicentennial (55 produced in 1976 only), Presentation in 1977–84, Waterfowl graded with 500 each of Mallard (1981), Pintail (1982) and Black Duck (1983), Classic and Gold Class (2,500 and 500 in 1986 only.)

Browning Custom Shop

High quality hand finishing and engraving are offered for all browning guns at the Browning Custom Shop in Herstal, Belgium. Barrel-making, boring, engraving, fitting out, assembly, stock making, checkering and finishing are all carried out by traditional craftsmen. The classic B25 superposed shotgun range is still the most popular subject

for custom treatment with over nineteen grades of finish available. Engraving is carried out to customer's special requirements; one customer recently had pictures of his Aston-Martin car on his lockplates!

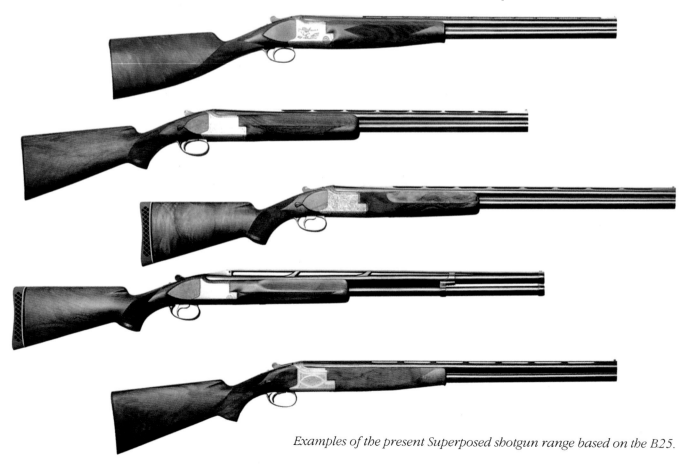

Examples of the present Superposed shotgun range based on the B25.

Classic Superposed shotgun built in 1966 with a 26.5 inch vent-rib barrel.

BROWNING SHOTGUNS TODAY

The Citori Lightning.

In the 21st century the Browning Arms Company continues to market shotgun designs which obviously take full advantage of the most modern advances in the fields of gun technology, metallurgy and manufacturing, but which, to a surprising extent, also embody the concepts – and in many case the actual design features – pioneered by the great John M. Browning over a century ago. Five main models are described here, but it must be borne in mind that within each of these models there are many minor variations.

The BT-99 single-barrel shotgun has been in the Browning line-up since 1969 and is now in its 36th continuous year of production. It is intended for trap shooting and is available in 12-gauge only, with 30-, 32- or 34-inch vent-ribbed barrels. Individual models have come and gone over the years and three were available

in 2006, comprising the BT-99 with or without an adjustable comb, BT-99 Golden Clays with adjustable comb, and the BT-99 Micro, which has a small frame and is somewhat lighter.

The Citori range has been made by Miroku in Japan since 1973 and features superposed, vent-ribbed barrels, in either 12- or 20-gauge, and in the usual wide range of finishes. There are a number of post-John Browning developments, including the hammer-blow ejectors which ensure a very positive ejection of spent shells, while the barrels are selected by a thumb-operated lever, giving the first pull on one, the second on the other. The trigger system includes three shoes and the ability for the shooter to adjust the length of pull with an Allen-key. The potential buyer is offered a choice of no less than 24 discrete models within the Citori range.

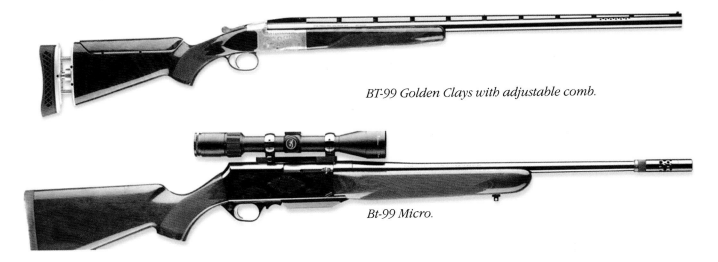

BT-99 Golden Clays with adjustable comb.

Bt-99 Micro.

The Gold Series

THE GOLD SERIES, introduced in 1993, is an automatic shotgun, which is available in at least 21 versions, in either 12- or 20-gauge, which are intended to meet almost every hunter's need. The barrels are either vent-ribbed, conventional or thick skinned, and range in length from 26 to 30 inches. The gas-operated action has a very short piston stroke and efficient design results in reduced wear in the receiver and piston, and a longer life. The tubular, under-barrel magazine houses either three or four shells, with all having one further shell in the chamber. In addition to the conventional finishes, the National Wild Turkey Federation (NWTF) series is camouflaged in a variety of elaborate break-up patterns.

Above: Gold Fusion High Grade Shotgun with carrying case and inset detail of engraving.

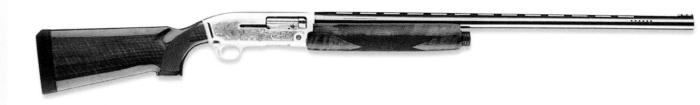

Above: Gold "Golden Clays" Ladies Sporting Clays.

Above: Gold Evolve in 12 gauge.

Above: Gold Light 10 gauge in Mossy Oak finish.

Above: Gold Micro.

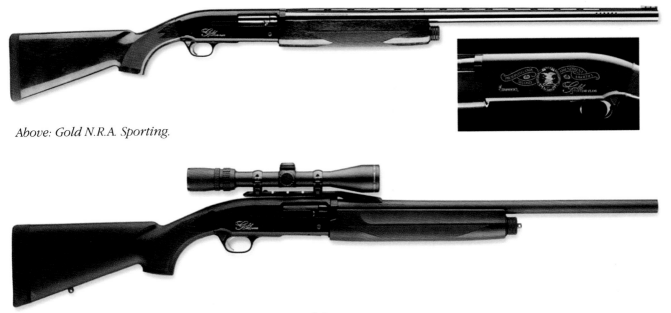

Above: Gold N.R.A. Sporting.

Above: Gold Rifles Deer Stalker [slug ammunition only].

The Cynergy Series

THE CYNERGY SERIES was introduced in 2004 and represents the third generation of superposed shotguns. While not being directly derived from Browning's original design the improvements incorporated in the Cynergy range of shotguns are in total harmony with his philosophy of constant innovation. Browning never let any of his designs become obsolete in his lifetime and would doubtless approve of the company continuing to modernize and improve the range on his behalf.

The monoblock hinge system reduces the gun's profile, the double reverse trigger improves handling, vent-ribbed barrels in either 12-, 20- or 28-gauge in a variety of lengths, a silver nitride receiver, and walnut or composition stock and forend. All versions of the Cynergy series are fitted with a specially designed recoil pad.

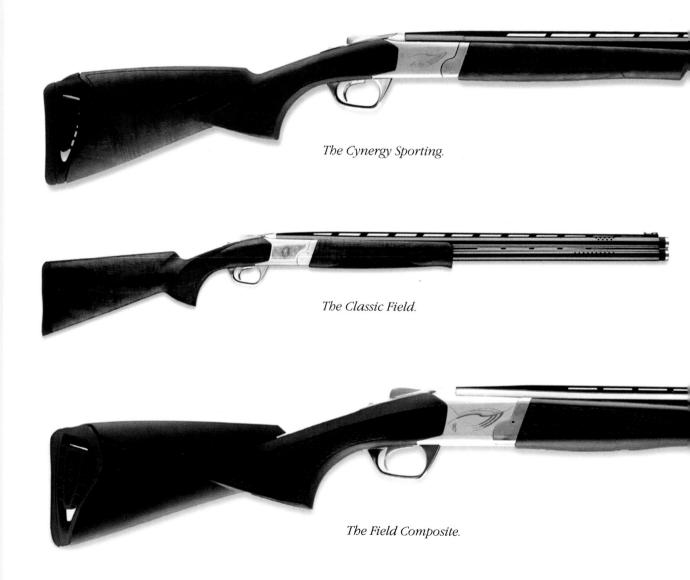

The Cynergy Sporting.

The Classic Field.

The Field Composite.

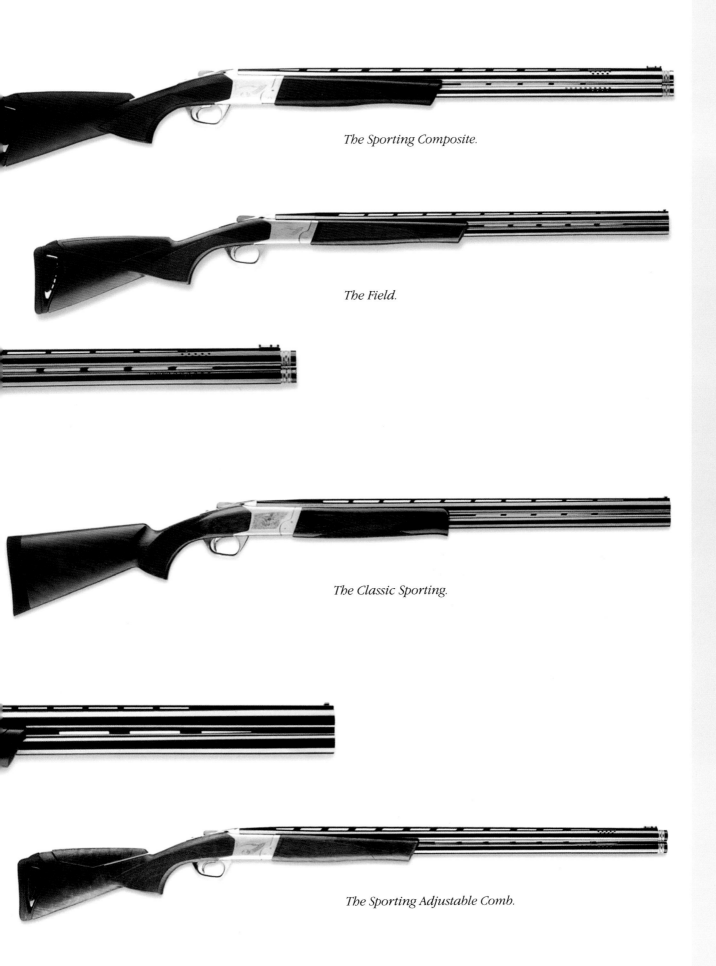

The Sporting Composite.

The Field.

The Classic Sporting.

The Sporting Adjustable Comb.

The BPS Series

THE BPS-SERIES (Browning Pump System) has been made by Miroku since 1978 and is a slide-operated sporting gun in 10-, 12-, or 20- gauge, with a five-shell under-barrel magazine and vent-ribbed barrels. The slide runs on double ribs to eliminate twisting and used shells are ejected from the bottom of the shotgun, keeping them clear of the shooter's line-of-sight and which, in combination with the pump-action, makes it truly ambidextrous. One of the unusual variants is the BPS Rifled Deer Hunter, which features a thick-walled, fully-rifled 22-inch barrel designed to fire slugs, and which is fitted with a cantilever mount for a telescopic sight, indicating a degree of accuracy, handiness and range which could make this particular weapon suitable for other than sporting uses.

Mossy Oak New Shadow Grass with Dura-Touch armor finish.

The BPS Slide-Action Shotgun made by B.C.Miroku.

BPS Hunter.

Rifled Deer Hunter.

Uplands Special.

CHAPTER FIVE

Browning Machine Guns

FROM THE 17TH CENTURY onwards many inventors searched for a method of producing automatic fire on the battlefield, the advantages of such a weapon, particularly in those days of massed armies in close-serried ranks fighting at very close ranges, being obvious. For many years the only possible way of achieving this was mechanically, i.e., by turning a handle which rotated a group of barrels or a magazine. One of the earliest pioneers was James Puckle, an Englishman, who took out a patent in 1718 for a gun with a single barrel and a chamber holding nine rounds, which was rotated by hand. Puckle's gun was not a success, but the pace quickened in the 19th century, with several inventors producing weapons with multiple barrels, grouped either radially or in rows which could be fired in quick succession. The best known of these was the Gatling gun, which had ten barrels rotated by means of a handle; it saw service in the United States during the Civil War and in the West, and with several foreign armies.

In the 1860s, the French invented the *Mitrailleuse* which had either 25 or 37 barrels firing 11 mm rounds either simultaneously or in rapid succession. Its capabilities were much vaunted by the French Army but it proved singularly ineffective when used by them in the Franco–Prussian war,

Richard J. Gatling's machine gun of 1862 had ten rotating barrels.

Above: Formal portait of John M. Browning with his Model 1895 automatic machine gun.

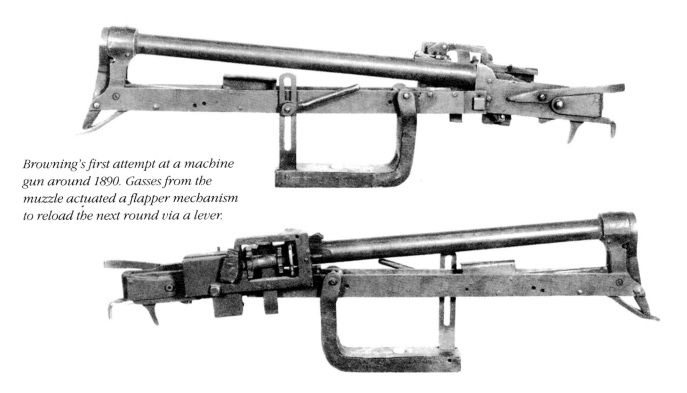

Browning's first attempt at a machine gun around 1890. Gasses from the muzzle actuated a flapper mechanism to reload the next round via a lever.

although this was due more to singularly inept tactical handling than to any technical shortcoming in the weapon itself. All of these multi-barrel weapons were mounted on horse-drawn artillery-style carriages with two large wheels, which encouraged those controlling them to look on them as artillery weapons rather than in direct support of infantry. Other mechanically-operated multi-barrel weapons were designed by men such as William Gardiner, an American, and Heldge Palmcrantz, a Swede, although the latter's weapons were more widely known by the name of the industrialist, Nordenfeld.

All these weapons used black powder in the cartridges, a disadvantage of which was that a cartridge could "hang fire" and suffer delayed ignition. This was a bad enough problem in a single-shot weapon, but such a cartridge firing after extraction had begun could be extremely dangerous in a mechanically-operated automatic.

Two Americans, John M. Browning and Hiram Maxim, quite independently of the other, saw the prospect of using the gasses from the firing cartridge to drive the gun's working parts to the rear and automatically load a further round, although they came to different conclusions as to how this was to be achieved. Maxim chose the recoil method and, having moved to England, sold his machine gun to the British and other European armies from 1884 onwards. Browning initially looked at a gas-powered system, and stayed at home in Ogden, Utah.

Browning experimental models

John Browning's first experimental model consisted of a Winchester rifle with the gasses actuating a small flap over the muzzle to recock the mechanism. Browning referred to this as an automatic magazine gun, and it was really a self-loading rifle rather than a machine gun; indeed, it was probably the first-ever such SLR. Browning obtained a United States patent (417,782/1892) for it, even though it was such a crude model that he can have had no intention of producing it.

Browning's next effort, the second experimental model, although still intended only for trials, was a genuine machine gun, capable of fully automatic fire. Again, this worked by using the energy at the muzzle, with a bracket secured here which carried a lever. The top end of the lever rested against the muzzle and had a .45 inch hole which allowed the bullet to pass through. The gasses which followed the bullet, however, expanded slightly as they left the muzzle and hit the lever with sufficient strength to push it forward, actuating a rod-and-lever assembly which extracted and then ejected the empty case, before feeding, loading and firing the next round from a cloth belt. The process was fully automatic and continued at a cyclic rate of 600 rounds per minute for as long as the trigger was pulled or there were rounds in the belt. The barrel was air-cooled and lacked any fins, so that it got very hot when fired continuously. Granted U.S. Patent 471,783/1892, this weapon was demonstrated first to the management at Colt and then to officers of the U.S. Navy. It proved very reliable and fully capable of meeting Browning's claims for it, but again it was what would be described in modern terms as a "proof-of-concept" model – indeed, it looked like a random assembly of pipes – and was not intended for production.

Browning's third experimental model (U.S. Patent 502,549/1893) took a new approach, with the flapper being replaced by tapping the gas before it reached the muzzle. Two holes were bored through the barrel walls, opposite each other, allowing the gas to escape to actuate a rod-and-lever assembly which was similar in principle to the earlier model. As soon as he tested the new weapon, however, Browning realized that he could obtain sufficient operating power and have a much simpler layout if he had just one hole in the bottom of the barrel.

Colt Model 1895 Automatic Machine Gun

Following the successful demonstrations of his second experimental model Browning developed a version suitable for production, which had one small port some 8 inches from the muzzle, enabling a small proportion of the gas to escape downwards. This activated a piston and drove a lever, which swung radially

The Colt –Browning Model 1895.

Lt Val Browning demonstrates the M1917 machine gun invented by his father John M. Browning.

back and forth through 90 degrees, one cycle for each round fired, and which, if the gun was too low, hit the ground, churning up the earth and earning it the nickname of "potato digger."

The weapon was air-cooled and tended to suffer from overheating. It was originally fitted with a thick-walled, smooth-sided barrel, and Colt's sales brochures claimed that cooling was aided by the swinging lever at the front acting as a pump to drive cold air over the barrel, but there is little evidence that this was anything other than marketing hype. Later models had a finned barrel to help dissipate the considerable heat, but it is doubtful that the overheating problem was ever fully solved.

The weapon was accepted, the initial buyer being the U.S. Navy, making this the first order placed by any of the U.S. armed forces for a fully automatic machine gun. An initial order for 50 was quickly followed by one for a further 150 and by 1900 the entire U.S. Navy and Marine Corps were equipped with the M1895. These were used with great success by the Marine Corps in the Boxer Rebellion in China and in the Spanish–American War. The Model 1895 was examined several times by the U.S. Army, but they declined to place an order, even when an updated version was produced as the M1904 and sold to various foreign armies. Among these was the Canadian Army which bought a small quantity, some of which were taken to France in 1915, although there is no record of them being used in battle.

Many of those bought by the U.S. Navy were still in service when the U.S. declared war on Germany in 1917 and since production facilities were available and Colt still had the necessary tools the M1895 was placed back in production, although, in the event, it was used almost exclusively as a training weapon.

The Model 1895 was chambered for either the .30-40 Krag or the 6 mm Lee rounds, which were fired at a cyclic rate of 400 rounds per minute. It was mounted on a low tripod, which was fully adjustable for bearing and elevation, and with a seat for the gunner, who controlled the gun using a pistol-type handgrip. The gun could not be fired dismounted from the tripod.

Colt Model 1917 .30 Caliber Machine Gun

John Browning's active mind was never idle and as soon as the M1895 machine gun had been accepted by Colt he started work on a new and even better weapon. His patent application was granted in 1901 but no production orders were forthcoming, so the project was put on hold, although he returned to it from time to time to make improvements. Thus, when the United States went to war in 1917, and despite all the information gleaned on the battles in Europe between 1914 and 1917 where the machine gun had proved its effectiveness time after

time, the army still found itself woefully short of such weapons. But, very fortunately, John M. Browning's new design was ready and after a very successful demonstration to members of the Congress, it was placed in immediate production as the Model 1917 by Colt, Remington and Westinghouse.

One of the outstanding characteristics of the Model 1917 was that, like so many of Browning's designs, it was mechanically very simple and straightforward, employing the short recoil principle and with a belt feed. The cycle started with the gunner pulling back and releasing the cocking handle, thus chambering a round and cocking the action. On firing, the recoil forced both barrel and breech-block to move backwards, locked together, for about half an inch, whereupon, the pressure having reduced to a safe level, the barrel released the breechblock, which then continued to the rear, compressing a spring, extracting the used case and ejecting it downwards, and drawing a new round from the belt. On hitting the buffer, the working parts were then propelled forwards by the return spring, chambering the new round, locking the breechblock and barrel together and then firing the new round. This firing sequence then continued until the gunner released the trigger or the belt was empty. Cooling was by means of a water jacket surrounding the barrel.

The Browning machine gun was produced in many versions, but all had the same basic mechanism, all were belt-fed, and all but one fired the .30-06 Springfield round. The sole exception was a U.S. Navy variant produced as late as the 1960s, which was modified to fire the 7.62 mm NATO round. The basic versions were designed for the infantry, tank and aircraft roles.

Infantry role.

The original infantry heavy machine gun was the tripod-mounted M1917 with a 24-inch barrel, as described above, which was followed in about 1930 by the M1917A1. This was originally produced in the 1920s at the Rock Island Arsenal by remanufacturing existing M1917s, but production later switched to new-builds. Compared to the M1917 this had modified cooling and a stronger feed mechanism, while bronze components were replaced by steel. This served many armies for many years to the Korea War and beyond.

The later air-cooled M1919A4 appeared for infantry use in 1934 and was a modified version of the tankers' M1919A2 (see below), but with a 24-inch barrel and improved belt-feed system, although it still used the same tripod as the M1919A2. The M1919A6 was the

Right: Stuart M5 Tank with a Browning M1919A5 mounted on top of the turret.

M1919A4 designed for use by the infantry as a light machine gun, with a shoulder stock, carrying-handle, flash hider and bipod. Like all other versions, this, too, used a 250-round cloth belt. It entered service in 1944.

Tank role

The first version for tanks was the M1919, which was similar to the M1917 but with a slotted jacket surrounding an air-cooled, 19-inch barrel, and a ball-mounting for installation in a turret, although the gun could also be dismounted and used with a tripod if necessary. This was followed in 1931 by two slightly improved versions for dismounted use by tank crews: the M1919A1 with a simple butt for use by tank corps crews, and the M1919A2 with no butt, different foresight and a heavier tripod. The A3 was an experimental model, while the A5 was produced specially for use in M3 General Stuart light tanks.

Left: The Browning M1919 was the main machine gun used by American Forces in World War II.

Aircraft role

Work started in 1917 to convert the M1917 water-cooled machine gun into a weapon suitable for use in aircraft. The result was the M1918, the first air-cooled version, in which the barrel was surrounded by a lightweight, slotted barrel jacket in place of the water-cooling of the M1917. This was designated M1918 Aircraft and was succeeded by a new-build weapon designated M1919 Aircraft in two versions: M1919 Fixed which was identical to the M1918, and M1919 Flexible which differed only in having spade grips and a pintle mounting. These guns were widely used in Allied aircraft during World War II. The British, for example, had their own versions, chambered for their .303 round, and used in fixed batteries in fighters – the famous Hurricane and Spitfires had eight each – and in the turrets of most of their bombers.

The .50 in Water-Cooled Heavy Machine Gun

As soon as U.S. forces arrived in France in 1917, their commander, General John Pershing, demanded a machine gun with a heavier, harder-hitting bullet than the .30-06 Springfield used by the M1917 machine gun. The first attempt to meet this urgent requirement was made by U.S. Ordnance experts in France, who adapted the M1917 to take the newly developed French 11 mm (.43 in) round, but this was doomed to failure. Further efforts in the United States to develop an

Above: The British Hawker Hurricane was fitted with eight forward-firing .303 in M1919 machine guns.

even heavier .50 in round also failed until John M. Browning was brought in. He, in effect, redesigned the new round first, and then designed a new weapon to fire it.

Browning started work in July 1917 and the prototype was under test by Colt just over a year later. It was a water-cooled weapon, in essence the M1917 design scaled up to handle the heavier round and with an oil buffer, also invented by John Browning, which absorbed the much greater energy from the new cartridge without any increase in weight. Unlike the M1917 which had a pistol grip, the .50 caliber had twin spade grips.

This new weapon passed all its tests but could not be

Above: The Browning 0.50 caliber M2 Machine gun.

put into production before World War I came to an end in November 1918. It was type tested as the M1921 and entered service with the U.S. Army in 1925, with a slightly modified version, the M1921A1 appearing in 1930. This water-cooled weapon was produced in vast numbers during World War II by nine U.S. companies and was also widely copied in other countries.

The .50 in Air-Cooled M2 Heavy Machine Gun

In 1933, some years after John Browning's death, a new air-cooled version of the M1921 appeared under the designation .50 in M2. This was intended originally for use in multiple mounts in aircraft, but there were also versions for use in tank turrets and on ground-mounted tripods. This worked in the same manner as the M1921, using John Browning's short recoil system, but, although it was mechanically reliable, the thin-walled barrel tended to overheat to such an extent that after some 70–80 rounds had been fired it was necessary to stop for a period to allow the barrel to cool. This problem was completely resolved by the development of a new barrel with much thicker walls, and the weapon, now designated the M2HB (for Heavy Barrel) became an absolute winner, being used by military forces throughout the world,

many of which are still very happy to retain it in service. It has been used in ground mounts, on wheeled vehicles, in tanks, and aboard ships, and was even used as a heavy sniping weapon during the Vietnam War. The M2HB is no lightweight, weighing in at 84 pounds for the gun and a further 44 pounds for the M3 tripod, plus more, of course, for the ammunition, but it is highly effective. The one problem with the original versions of the M2HB was that a barrel change had to be followed by adjustments to the headspace, as even a few thousandths of an inch could effect the efficiency of the firing process; this was not difficult using the gauges supplied, but it took a little time, which was not always available in battle.

The M2 can be mounted on the ground (tripod), in vehicles, tanks, aircraft or ships. It is fitted with an adjustable leaf-type rear sight, and the 45-inch barrel has a flash suppressor; a spare barrel is always supplied. Ammunition can be fed from left or right, changeover being quick and simple, with ammunition being fed by a disintegrating metallic-link belt. Most versions are capable of full automatic fire only, but ground-mounted guns have also have a single-shot capability.

The M2HB has been developed over the years, although the basic mechanism, as designed by John M. Browning, remains unchanged. A quick-change barrel (QCB) kit was introduced to overcome the headspace adjustment problem, and efforts have also been made to reduce the weight.

The M2HB remains in service with at least 30 armed forces, including the U.S. Army, and as recently as July 2005 the U.S. Army's Tank Automotive Command started taking delivery of an order for 1,151 new-build M2HBs. Thus, the M2HB, with its range of 2,000 yards and a rate-of-fire of 450 rounds per minute remains in full production some 80 years after John Browning completed its design.

Browning M1918 Automatic Rifle (BAR)

Many designers of military equipment produce new designs in response to requirements stated by the military authorities, but John M. Browning, despite his lack of any personal combat experience, was able to look ahead and anticipate the future needs of the military with astonishing accuracy. Thus, in 1910 he started to design a weapon that is known to history as the Browning Automatic Rifle (BAR), although today it would be called, in its original form, an assault rifle, and in its later form, when fitted with a bipod, as a light machine gun (LMG) or squad automatic weapon (SAW).

Clyde Barrow was an enthusiast of Browning weapons particularly the Browning Automatic Rifle.

Browning completed and demonstrated the prototypes, but neither the U.S. Army nor the Marine Corps had an immediate requirement for such a weapon. As a result, the design remained at Ogden, where Browning bided his time, revisiting it periodically and improving it on each occasion.

As a result, when, in February 1917 and less than two months before committing itself to the war in Europe, the United States Army suddenly called for just such a weapon, John Browning and the BAR were ready. The BAR was light enough (16 pounds) to be carried by an individual infantryman, and could be fired from the shoulder or the hip (there was no bipod until later); it had a cyclic rate of 480 rounds per minute and could be fired in either full automatic or single-shot modes from its bottom-feeding magazine, using the same .30-06 Springfield service round as the riflemen. Not only was it revolutionary in design, it was also very user-friendly and could be stripped down to its 70 components in just 55 seconds. The BAR was demonstrated to members of Congress and government officials on February 27, 1917 and ordered into immediate production, but to avoid confusion with the M1917 water-cooled machine gun, it was designated the M1918.

Approximately 50,000 were produced before the war ended in November 1918 and they were used with great success by U.S. troops in the final months of the war, where John Browning's eldest son, Lieutenant Val Browning, had the honor of being the first to use it in action. It was gas-operated, with the gas being led off by a tap underneath the barrel to a gas piston and fired from the open-bolt position, in either automatic (550 rounds per minute) or semi-automatic modes. The 20-round magazine was mounted below the gun and on rapid fire could be emptied in about 2.5 seconds. The overall weight of the gun and its ammunition made it difficult to fire with any hope of accuracy from the standing shoulder position, while the low firing position meant that a larger magazine could not be fitted, nor was there any means of adapting the gun to belt feed. Nevertheless, the BAR was extremely reliable – John Browning's designs always were – and enjoyed a high reputation with the troops that used it, always a key factor in a weapon's success.

Production continued after the war in both the U.S. (by Colt) and abroad. Fabrique Nationale in Belgium designated it the M30 *Fusil Mitrailleur Léger* and sold it to the Belgian army (7.65 mm), Chilean army (7 mm) and Chinese army (7.92 mm). Fabrique Nationale also produced a developed version, the Type D, with various improvements including a bipod, which was supplied to the Belgian army (.30-05) and Egypt (7.02 mm). It was also manufactured in Poland as the Radom M28 (7.92 mm), and in Sweden by the Carl Gustav factory as the M21 and improved M37, both in 6.55 mm Mauser caliber.

The BAR also continued in production in the United States. The M1922 was produced in the early 1920s for the U.S. Cavalry (still horsed at that time) and was very similar to the M1918 except for a finned barrel to improve cooling, better sights and a bipod. The M1918A1 appeared in 1927, the main change being a bipod attached to the gas cylinder, thus converting the gun into a light machine gun, and a small butt strap which could be swiveled through 90 degrees so that the weapon could rest on the gunner's shoulder, this maintaining the firing position but enabling the gunner to use his hands for other tasks. When not in use the strap was folded forward to lie snug against the butt plate. The bipod solved the accuracy problem, although, somewhat paradoxically, at its maximum effective range of about 1,000 yards the BAR was now almost too accurate for a machine gun since the beaten zone was so small. Indeed, many years later, in Vietnam, some units mounted BARs on high and heavily protected platforms and employed them as long-range sniper weapons.

The M1918A2, introduced in 1939, had further advances including a flash hider, better sights and a rate-of-fire adjuster, which enabled the gunner to fire at either 450 or 650 rounds per minute, although it deleted

Above: Browning Automatic Rifle with bipod.

the semi-automatic mode. On this model the bipod swivel was moved forward to the muzzle end of the barrel. By now the weight was up to 19 pounds 8 ounces and during the war a carrying handle and pistol grip were introduced.

Unfortunately, the M1918 BAR was also put to another use during the years between World Wars I and II, when it proved attractive to a number of the more notorious gangsters of the era, including John Dillinger and Clyde Barrow (of Bonnie and Clyde fame). Such criminals obtained their BARs in raids on police and National Guard armories, and often shortened the barrel and cut down the stock so that the weapon could be concealed under a coat. On the law-and-order side, Colt produced the Colt Monitor for police and security guards, which was a BAR with a shortened (18-inch) barrel, pistol grip and other refinements, the most visually obvious of which was the Cutts compensator, a large cylindrical device fitted to the muzzle. The Colt Monitor proved popular with the FBI, Texas Rangers and a number of prison authorities, all of whom found it more reliable and effective than its contemporary, the Thompson sub-machine gun.

The total number of BARs of all types produced in the United States was about 350,000, to which must be added those produced in Belgium, Poland and Sweden, making a total somewhere in the region of 400,000. That is, however, not the end of the story as in the 1990s Ohio Ordnance Works introduced a new weapon, which they designate the Browning M1918A3, which replicates the external appearance of the BAR but with some elements of the receiver and working parts improved and updated, many of which are produced by computer-controlled machines rather than by traditional methods. The only real disadvantages to the BAR were the lack of a quick-change barrel, its weight, and the small number of rounds in the underslung magazine. Against this, for some 50 years the rifle squad in both the U.S. Infantry and the Marine Corps was organized around one or more BARs, weapons which had an outstanding reputation for reliability and effective fire.

Above: A cutaway of the M30 Fusil Mitrailleur Léger (FN-made BAR).

Browning Knives

IN COMMON WITH OTHER major gun companies, the Browning Arms Company have developed a range of edged tools and weapons to suit the outdoor hunting, fishing and survival market. We show here a variety of knives for different purposes, although this only a section of the range. Most are strictly practical tools although there are also some beautifully finished and engraved items intended for collectors.

Sheath

Buckhorn, olive, drop point with guthook

This fixed blade knife has a Teflon-coated steel blade, sculpted olive wood handle and Italian leather sheath. An ideal knife for hunting and fishing.

Scorpion tanto knife

This knife features a folding lock back blade in 420 HC steel with a hard anodized 6061-T6 aircraft-grade aluminum handle for extra durability. Complete with pocket clip and thumbstud for easy opening.

Eclipse folding liner lock knife

Features a Teflon-coated blade engraved with John M. Browning's signature and an olive wood handle. A handy and distinctive pocket knife for general use.

Sliver green

A folding locking liner with a bead-blasted laser engraved 420 high carbon steel blade, hard anodized 6061-T6 aircraft grade aluminum handle and stainless steel skeletonized pocket clip. Attractive green anodized finish makes this a good-looker.

Elite signature knife

A fixed drop point blade in Teflon-coated 440 C stainless steel. The knife features a Zytel handle with rubber inlay and a distinctive contrasting red Buckmark logo. It has a lanyard fixing for extra security and a sheath made from ballistic cloth.

Wind River skinner

A very useful survival tool that has a scratch-resistant Teflon-coated 440 C blade, laser engraved with the Browning logo. The handle comes in Mossy Oak and has a ballistic cloth sheath with leather trim.

Wind River axe

An essential all-purpose survival tool which offers both a chopping edge as well as a billhook edge. Available with either Mossy Oak or plain aluminum handle.

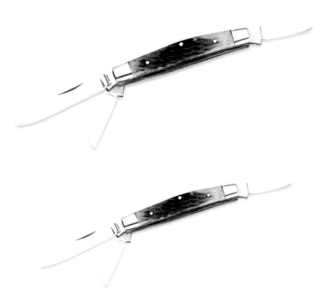

Amber bone traditional pocket knives

A folding knife with blades in AUS-8A steel featuring traditional amber bone handles.

A classic-looking knife that is ideal for everyday use for people who just like to have knife handy, or for serial knife collectors! We show one example with three blades, the other with two.

Living History knives

This collectors' series commemorates significant events in the history of the United States, and each one is produced as a limited edition cleverly numbered to align with the year of the event. They are aimed at the collectors market rather than for practical use.

The Alamo knife

A limited edition of 1836 to mark the Battle of the Alamo, where 200 brave Americans fought the might of Santa Anna's Army massed at the gates. Davey Crockett and Jim Bowie both perished in the struggle.

The handle of the knife is hand-turned from wood from a giant oak still growing in the Alamo grounds. The 14-inch blade is hand-forged over a 10-day period from high carbon steel. The blade is engraved with tributes to the men who died, together with a single gold star that symbolizes the emblem of Texas, and with the words "Give me Help, Oh my Country."

The Vietnam knife

A limited edition of 1975 to commemorate the year the war ended. The knife is based on a special forces design favored by the MACV-SOG group, whose distinctive logo appears inside the box. The handle is crafted from Khan Hin wood from along the Ho Chi Minh Trail.

Index

Acknowledgments

The publishers would like to thank the following for their help in preparing this book.
Robert Sauvage, Herstal Group.
Pascal Pruvost, New Look Communications.
Paul Thompson, Browning.
Patrick F. Hogan, Rock Island Auction Company.
Roy Marcot, hunters images.
Mike Rose, Hawker Hurricane and Stuart M5 Tank.
Audrey and George Delange for the pictures of reconstructed Nauvoo.
Major Conway, S.A.S.C. Weapons Room.
The LDS Church Archive.
Union Pacific Railroad Museum.